The Distributed Development Environment

The Distributed Development Environment

The art of using CASE

UNICOM

APPLIED INFORMATION TECHNOLOGY REPORTS

Edited by **Simon Holloway**

Principal Consultant, DCE Information Management Consultancy Ltd

CHAPMAN AND HALL

LONDON · NEW YORK · TOKYO · MELBOURNE · MADRAS

UK   Chapman and Hall, 2–6 Boundary Row, London SE1 8HN

USA   Van Nostrand Reinhold, 115 5th Avenue, New York NY10003

JAPAN   Chapman and Hall Japan, Thomson Publishing Japan, Hirakawacho Nemoto
              Building, 7F, 1–7–11 Hirakawea-cho, Chiyoda-ku, Tokyo 102

AUSTRALIA   Chapman and Hall Australia, Thomas Nelson Australia, 102 Dodds Street,
              South Melbourne, Victoria 3205

INDIA   Chapman and Hall India, R. Seshadri, 32 Second Main Road, CIT East,
              Madras 600 035

First edition 1990

© 1990 UNICOM Seminars Ltd

Printed in Great Britain by T. J. Press (Padstow) Ltd., Padstow, Cornwall

ISBN 0–412–37820–5   0–442–31293–8 (USA)

British Library Cataloguing in Publication Data
The distributed development environment : the art of using
CASE. — (UNICOM applied information technology reports).
1. Computer systems. Software. Development. Applications
of computer systems
I. Holloway, Simon   II. Series
005.1

ISBN 0–412–37820–5

Library of Congress Cataloging-in-Publication Data
The Distributed development environment: the art of using CASE /
edited by Simon Holloway.
      p.   cm.   — (Unicom applied information technology reports)
      ISBN 0–442–31293–8
      1. Computer-aided software engineering.   2. Electronic data
processing—Distributed processing.   I. Holloway, Simon.
II. Series.
QA76.758.D57   1990   90–2084
005.1—dc20   CIP

CONTENTS

Contributors

Mr Richard Barker
Vice President, CASE
Oracle Corporation (UK) Ltd

Mr Tim Bourne
Stradard Information Analysis Methods Ltd

Dr John Burke
Principal Consultant
SD-Scicon

Mr Bob Grover
Principal Consultant CASE Tools Division
Hoskyns Group plc

Mr Simon Holloway
Principal Consultant
DCE Information Management Consultancy Ltd

Professor Darrel Ince
Department of Computing
Faculty of Mathematics
Open University

Mr Russell Jones
Editor
"Software Development Monitor"

Mr Manjeet Khaira
SSADM Research Centre
Department of Computing
City of Birmingham Polytechnic

Mr Jon Lansdell
Bacchus and Smith Ltd

Mr Gerrard Lennox
CONSENSUS

Mr Bob Mcgee
Independant Consultant

Mr David Piesse
Managing Director
Azimuth Software Ltd

Mr Geoffrey Rose
SCOLL

Mr Brian Strowger
Information Systems Engineering Division
CCTA

Dr Richard Williams
Richalis Computer Services Ltd

Dr Sami Zahran
Senior Management Consultant
Digital Equipment Company Ltd

Part One

CASE: Present and Near Future

1
REVIEW OF CURRENT CASE TECHNOLOGIES

Russell Jones
Editor "Software Development Monitor".

1 INTRODUCTION

Rarely has a technology gained such a rapid foothold in the minds of IS professionals as CASE has. Although the exact meaning of CASE - is it computer-aided software engineering or computer-aided systems engineering - remains under debate, there is no doubt that the central messages of the technology are now firmly implanted in the minds of IS developers.

From a point three or four years ago where, to misquote James Martin, IS staff were still "subject to the tyranny of the template and the coding pad", CASE now represents perhaps the major software market for the IS industry, with a projected market size of between $600 million and $1 billion in 1982.

2 CASE: THE BASICS

CASE attempts to "automate the automators" by providing tools to support as many elements of the software development process as is feasible. This means that CASE tools are emerging to support the accepted software lifecycle phases: analysis, design, "code cutting", implementation, and maintenance.

Its worth pointing out that, certainly at the analysis and design levels, CASE can have no real meaning other than within a methodology context. Or to put it another way: CASE is designed primarily to automate the techniques that go to make up modern development methodologies.

Although the CASE industry has thus far been rather longer on promises than on actual delivery, it is already feasible to list the benefits that seem likely to follow from the use of CASE:

- it makes feasible, and acts as an agent of contagion for, structured development techniques;

- it enforces the use by IS staff of the standards inherent in good development methodologies;

- it improves software quality by enabling users to act as "arbiters of the final resort" of that quality;

- it encourages the use of prototyping during detail design and development;

- it reduces program maintenance - both in the short term and the long term;

- it speeds elements of the development process;

- it frees IS developers from drudgery, enabling them to concentrate on the business aspects of development.

At the moment much of the interest in the CASE market revolves around boosting the speed of software developers. In reality however, the most far reaching result of CASE is likely to be a radical improvement in the quality of software.

CASE forces developers to adhere more closely to good methodological practice. Paradoxically, this seems likely to increase the amount of time taken to develop any given piece of software.

The productivity payoff will come in the long term. Well engineered, quality assured software requires far less maintenance. So it's important for those assessing the potential of CASE to take a long term view of the productivity improvements the technology makes feasible.

3   SHORT HISTORY OF CASE

The software development environment has evolved slowly over the last thirty years, and can be characterised as follows:

- early 1960s standalone development

- late 1960s batch development

- late 1970s time sharing

- late 1980s personal workstations

- early 1990s PC-based work group development

Clearly, CASE tools sit at the vanguard of the movement towards the use of developer workstations, in both standalone and workgroup mode. Indeed, hardly any of the currently popular CASE tools would exist, had the PC not been invented.

In fact the arrival of the PC, is one of the two historical keys to CASE development. The other is the emergence of a family of highly structured methods for systems analysis and design.

Early pioneers the CASE market, notably Index Technology and Nastec, built tools that exploited the power of the new PCs to automate the drawing of the diagrams to be found within structured techniques.

Gradually it became apparent that simply changing the ubiquitous template for a mouse, simply wasn't enough. It became necessary to store, not the diagrams that analysts drew, but the objects that made up those diagrams.

Newer CASE tools, notably from vendors such as James Martin Associates (JMA), Oracle and Knowledgeware, introduced the concept of a central repository of design information. Diagrams became "windows" into that repository, rather than entities in their own right.

Nearly all early CASE tools concentrated on automating the tasks of systems analysts. Latterly however, CASE tools have started to support related lifecycle tasks:

- strategic systems planning;

- detailed systems design;

- code generation;

- systems maintenance;

- various types of reverse engineering.

4   A CASE LINCHPIN: REPOSITORY

As the scope of CASE tools has broadened to encompass more and more of the software lifecycle, so the importance of the repository has grown. Not only does the modern day repository act as a developer's database, it also forms the basis for automatic code generation.

In the future, the repository will also increasingly act as a "target" for reverse engineering tools looking to extract design abstractions from existing code.

In addition, it is possible that Integrated Project Support Environments (IPSEs) will utilise the repository to store various types of project control and management, and versioning information.

5   A TAXONOMY OF CURRENT CASE TOOLS

More than one approach has been taken by CASE vendors to building automated support for IS developers. As a result, a variety of different types of tools have emerged, and are still emerging.

Broadly speaking, CASE tool can be divided up into four wide categories, according to their ancestry. The categories are:

5.1 Workbenches

These derive from the automation of structured methods for planning, analysis, design and coding. Typically, a workbench support for the trio of "must have" analysis diagrams: entity relationship, decomposition, dataflow. Other diagram types typically depend on how closely aligned a CASE tool is to any one methodology. Some tools, notably JMA's Information Engineering Facility (IEF) split elements of functionality between workstations and a central computer. Other tools, for example LBMS's Automated Plus, market as workstation-only tools.

Purpose Of Workbench:

Define system requirements and properties system must possess to meet these requirements.

Output:

System specification of system components and interfaces connecting these components.

Screen, report definitions, data structures, databases and files, functional components.

Workbench Facilities:

Diagramming tools: dataflow etc.

Prototyping tools: screen and report painters, executable specification language.

Information repository with reporting capability.

Import/export capabilities between repository and outside dictionaries.

5.2 Integrated Project Support Environments (IPSE)

These products originally derived from software project management needs, and from software specification and project control methods. Typically, IPSEs provide the sort of project control facilities that most CASE tools currently lack, for example: project planning and management facilities, configuration management tools, versioning capabilities.

Typical IPSE Facilities:

Word processing.

Interface to electronic mail.

Project management.

Configuration management for version and access control.

Project planning.

Calendar and task assignment system.

Estimator tool.

Timetables and scheduling tools.

Quality control metrics.

Case repository with system audit trail.

5.3 Application generation tools

These are derived from DBMS, 4GL and related areas, and from code generators. These tools offer the same basic facilities as a "professional" 4GL, typically: a screen painter, a report generator, a way of generating "skeleton" code. Others also include minimal help for turning first cut designs into detailed designs optimised for specific environments. The most successful product, notably Pansophic's Telon, Sage's APS and ICL's QuickBuild, generate Cobol source code that then has to be compiled in the normal manner. Again typically, an application generator accesses a repository of some sort to gain access to the design objects that form the basis of code generation.

Typical Output of Application Generator:

> Source code;
>
> Database/file definitions and JCL.

Typical Facilities of Application Generator:

> Screen and report painter.
>
> Prototyping support.
>
> Data modelling and data dictionary.
>
> Procedural logic handling and database access.
>
> Code and documentation generator.
>
> Specification manager to store program specifications.
>
> Testing/debugging tools.
>
> Import/export to external databases and dictionaries.

5.4 Reverse engineering tools

These cover a number of approaches to the analysis of existing systems and to the restructuring of existing code to improve both form and execution efficiency. Sub-categories in this area include:

Software Resource Analysis Tools

These tools are marketed on the basis that, before a programmer can actually alter program code, he or she must spend much time working out which code to alter. Software analysis tools offer a way of building comprehensive module/program/job step/job cross references. More advanced capabilities include the assessment of the complexity of programs - in terms of the processing they are trying to achieve - and of the degree to which individual programs can be considered to be well structured.

Code Restructuring Tools

The restructuring process is based upon a number of key, well accepted, software engineering principles: the fundamental constructs of structured programs - that is sequence, selection and iteration; the structure theorem and the mathematics behind structured programming: the method of converting unstructured programs to structured ones.

Leading restructuring tools, notably IBM's Restructuring Facility, Language Technology (LTI)'s Recoder and Catalyst's Structured Retrofit, analyse the basic structure of a program, reorganise it into well recognised constructs without altering the logical consistency of the program, and regenerate code, including as many of the original program's "landmarks" as possible.

True Reverse Engineering Tools

Here, we're moving into futures, because, with the well publicised exception of the Bachman tool for reverse engineering definitions from IMS and IDMS into DB2, no real reverse engineering tools exist yet. The hope here is that tools will emerge that are capable of abstracting the "business logic" essence of a program direct from its code. The abstracted logic will be placed in a central CASE repository, where developers can meld it with design information gleaned during a normal "forward engineering" process of analysis and design. The whole will then be used as the basis of new applications.

6   ESSENTIAL CHARACTERISTICS OF CASE TOOLS

Although there are some mainframe and mini-based CASE tools, most CASE products rely upon the use of powerful PC workstations (although some products also use DEC and Sun workstations).

CASE tends to exploit the power of a PC to the utmost, and successive generations of CASE tools have used more and more processing power. For example the first version of Knowledgeware's Information Engineering Workbench (IEW) required 1.5 Mb of RAM storage, at a time when hardly any PC users routinely worked with more than 512K RAM. Today, a leading edge CASE tool, like the Bachman reverse engineering toolset, already requires ultra high resolution graphics and a minimum of 16 Mb RAM.

All CASE tools exploit mouse technology, and an increasing number of CASE products are based around standard windowing techniques, such as IBM's Presentation Manager, Microsoft's Windows, or DEC's X-Windows.

Individual vendors have used their own repository as a means of integrating various components within one CASE tool. For example, IEW has three or four notionally separate component products, but all interface directly to the IEW repository.

Integration between tools from different vendors is far more difficult to achieve. It is typically implemented via, fairly simplistic, batch transfers between so called "front-end" CASE tools (such as Automate, Excelerator and IEW) and so called "back-end" tools (such as Telon and APS).

For the future, the hope is that a standard repository will emerge that all vendors will interface to. Leading the way in this regard are Pansophic with PAN/RD, and Philips/Softlab with a new object oriented repository for the Maestro II IPSE.

The emergence of an industry-standard repository seems unlikely at the moment. ANSI and ISO flatly disagree in this area. A far more likely scenario is for IBM to announce a DB2-based repository, which will turn into a *de facto* industry standard.

CASE may be one of the first areas in IS where expert systems capabilities will be used actively to support the work of software developers. Already a few tools, notably again IEW, use some AI techniques during the checking of analysis and design information entered by software developers. In effect this offers developers a more rigorous way of checking their input for errors.

But the future use of AI within CASE tools seems certain to follow the pattern set by the Bachman reverse engineering toolset. This acts as a "true" expert system for IS staff, in that it actively and intelligently guides the developer through the reverse engineering process.

In the future, many more CASE tools will come complete with "embedded domain knowledge" about various aspects of the software lifecycle.

7   METHODOLOGY COVERAGE

As far as methodology coverage is concerned, CASE tools fall broadly into one of two categories: "church" or "religion". The latter are usually sold by vendors who also market a methodology; the former usually attempt to support a whole range of the techniques found within a number of different methodologies.

A new category of CASE tool is also emerging, perhaps best typified by Systematica's Virtual Software Factory. These are essentially "church" CASE tools. But they enable users to build their own methodology "priests". So, for example, Virtual Software Factory provides a whole range of generic diagramming tools which users can customise in order to use them to represent the particular objects manipulated within their particular methodology.

In general, methodology-specific CASE tools have produced the best results so far, in that users have been able to leverage the tools' methodology content to impose standards hitherto missing within the development process.

In the longer term however, it seems likely that methodology-unspecific CASE tools will become the norm, with vendors providing ever increasingly powerful facilities to enable users to customise those tools for specific environments.

8   WHO MARKETS CASE TOOLS ?

The CASE market is one area of computing where a real diversity of vendors exists, including hardware manufacturers, generic software vendors, methodology specialists, and start-up CASE vendors.

12

Hardware vendors are not yet major players in the CASE market. But that's not to say that they have no role at all to play - indeed, a vendor like ICL dominates the software tools market on its own hardware. But it does mean that, by and large, hardware vendors have thus far proven ill-equipped to react nimbly enough to the opportunities that new software development technologies offer up.

That said, there are a few key product types where the role of the hardware vendor is still very important. For example, IBM seems sure to attempt to dominate the CASE market by establishing a *de facto* standard with its promised repository.

The CASE market supports a number of vendors who have made their name by attempting to market a broad generic range of software tools. For example, Pansophic markets a large number of products, most of which are designed to aid in some way the development of IS software, and it is attempting to make a major impact in the CASE market.

Methodology vendors, such as Arthur Young, JMA, Arthur Andersen and LBMS, have been very important early players in the CASE market. Indeed, it is arguable that the products marketed by these specialists currently offer the most functionality to prospective purchasers.

However, despite the presence of hardware and software vendors, and methodology specialists, it is relatively young companies which, by and large, continue to dominate the burgeoning CASE market. Vendors such as Index Technology, Knowledgeware and Sage are mere minnows in the computer industry, yet the software tools that they market occupy a central role in the computer strategies of a growing number of commercial organisations.

9 CASE CHOICE –
MOVING TOWARDS THE DEVELOPER WORKSTATION

As might be expected, the choice of CASE tools available to IS developers is largest in the IBM market, with the DEC market following a fair distance behind. As noted earlier, ICL dominates the CASE market on its own hardware, although there is also a strong presence from LBMS and Philips. Similarly, there is a relatively small choice of CASE tools on Bull and Unisys hardware.

But the concept of CASE for a particular hardware environment is somewhat misplaced. That's because CASE really paves the way towards the developer workstation concept.

A number of CASE vendors - or, at least, two or more CASE vendors working together - now offer complete, PC-based, environments which developers can exploit in performing analysis and design aimed at producing a logical design of any proposed application. At the end of the design phase, a developer can then choose to turn that logical design into a physical design for any one of a number of target hardware and/or operating system environments.

Key to cooperation between vendors is the repository concept. Already, a "front-end" CASE tool, such as LBMS's Automate Plus, can populate its repository with hardware-independent design information. Then, a "back-end" application generation product, like Sage's APS, can utilise this information in generating applications for a specific hardware environment.

At the moment, that sort of link up is achieved via some sort of *ad hoc* batch transfer between separate repositories. For the future, the hope is that a common repository will act as the linking agent.

2

DICTIONARIES AND CASE:
CASE STANDARDS

Tim Bourne
Structured Information Analysis Methods Limited

1   INTRODUCTION

In view of the number of different interpretations of the term CASE, we begin by clarifying its use in the present paper. Computer Aided Software Engineering (CASE) is here taken to include any activity which employs the computer to assist in the effective and efficient production of computer-based solutions to business problems. These business problems may range from operational needs such as order processing or weapons control right through to providing information to support strategic decision making.

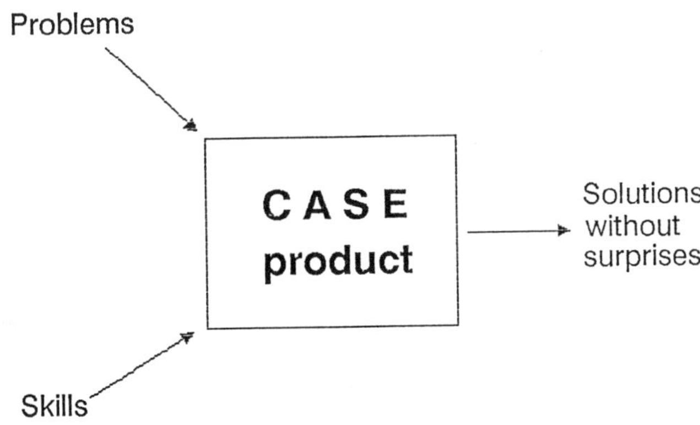

Figure 2.1 : What is CASE?

This scope includes many existing software products: compilers, database management systems, data dictionaries, project management systems and so on. All of these aid the software development process, all are computer-based, and all must be considered in any comprehensive solution. This introduces a point which will recur later: the key to successful application of CASE products will be the degree to which different products can be made to work well together.

Because of the different philosophies they bring to the CASE arena, it may be helpful first to consider the three principal origins of CASE products. These can be broadly categorised as mainframe data dictionaries, PC-based graphics tools, and mini-based workstations.

The mainframe system starts with an awareness of traditional DP problems and well-tried solutions to them. It also brings a tradition of "user-hostile" interfaces, and software which is ponderous and unresponsive. Graphics facilities are usually non-existent. However, this is the environment for which many software systems must be developed. In a number of instances ranges of products are now being developed around a data dictionary which can reasonably claim to be delivering CASE.

The PC offers graphics, and individual control and access, but at a price. There are now several good analysis and specification support tools available on PCs and Macs. These show that this aspect of software engineering can indeed be given effective support. Again, though, there is a catch: unless the desired system will run on a PC, the development work must then be transferred to another machine, and maintenance may require the use of both environments.

Thirdly, we have seen the growth of dedicated CASE workstations, often based on desktop minis running UNIX. This is certainly a convenient environment for research, and very effective if that is also the target system environment. The sceptical DP manager, though, may be forgiven for doubting whether anything coming from this alien environment has any relevance to his problems.

What we have to find, it seems, is some way of enabling the development process to exploit effectively the strengths of each of these types of system, while ensuring that the whole process can be tightly managed, with no uncontrolled data redundancy.

2   WHAT DO WE NEED?

Going back one step, let us consider what the typical potential user of CASE would like it to do for him. The following list of DP management problems is distilled from many discussions with development staff around the world, and is probably fairly typical:

- badly-specified requirements, leading to disagreement with the users when the system is delivered, and expensive changes after implementation;

- shortage of skilled resources, coupled with the fact that much of the development process, particularly in the early stages, is labour-intensive;

- expensive maintenance of existing systems, both because the original specification was wrong and because no adequate documentation exists;

- a diversity of PCs, minis and mainframes to support, sometimes with essentially the same system running in all three environments;

- unmanageable projects, leading to missed deadlines and total loss of credibility with users and senior management.

To solve these problems, what must CASE offer?

Fundamentally, it must attack the management problem. In the minds of most people, "engineering" implies control. Any computer-based aids must include inbuilt control mechanisms. In this context we should also recognise that the use of a variety of unrelated CASE products will probably do more harm than good. We will need a single product, or more likely a range of products, covering the whole of the development process, including the earliest planning stages. If more than one product is used, we will require easy and safe sharing of data between them.

How should the software engineering process be aided? Here we can learn from the experience of other branches of engineering: the priority should be to make skilled resources more productive, not to attempt the impossible goal of making them unnecessary. This applies particularly to maintenance; when a requirement changes, we need ways of assessing all the implications before deciding on a course of action.

Above all, we must remember that we are in effect talking about a database, not just about tools. There is no way that separate and unrelated tools can solve our problems. We must therefore bear in mind, in considering our requirements for CASE products, all we have learnt over the years about the successful application of the database principle (Figure 2.2).

> *"Each item of data should be captured once only, as close as possible to its source, and then stored in such a way as to be conveniently available to all people and systems with a legitimate need for access to it."*

Figure 2.2 : The database principle

Perhaps the most important lesson we have learnt is that thorough data analysis must precede database design, and that this analysis must cover more than just the immediate requirement. There is a real danger that users will become committed to a variety of CASE tools which have inconsistent underlying models of their data, thus preventing later consolidation in a single shared database. We must also insist that the implementors of CASE products follow existing standards where these are available, rather than reinventing the wheel. Relevant international standards already exist or are under development in the fields of database, data transfer, information resource dictionary systems (IRDS), and graphics.

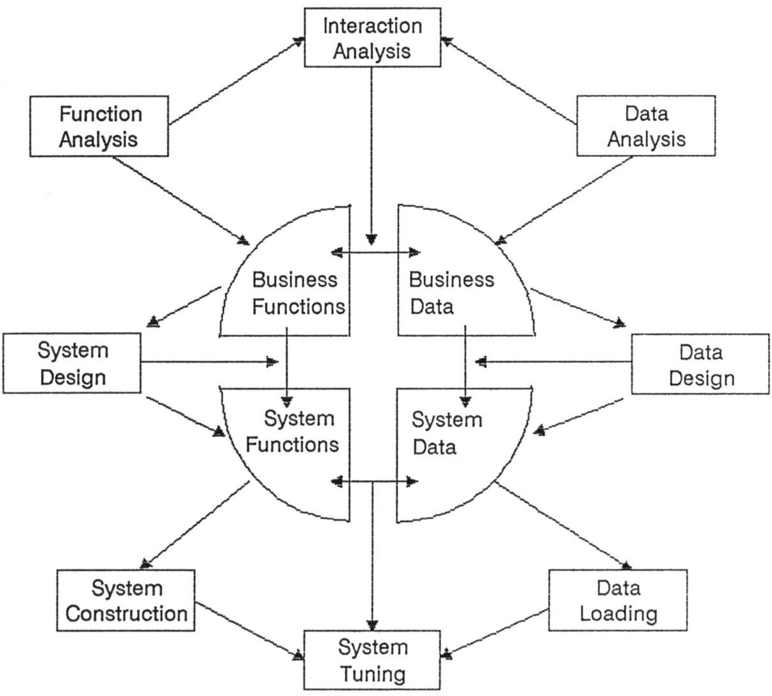

Figure 2.3 : The CASE dictionary

Figure 2.3 illustrates the way the dictionary (or "systems encyclopaedia") should become the centre around which all software engineering activity revolves. We can now examine the role of standards in making this possible.

3   WHY STANDARDS?

As we have seen, it is likely that most users will find the need to use two or more CASE tools to cover their requirements completely. Tools tend to be most effective when they are sharply focussed on a particular need; we have all seen products which can do many things, but none of them well! As in many other industries, the most effective product comes from a supplier who has identified a specific and well-defined need, who has the relevant practical experience to understand the problem and how it may be solved, and who specifies and produces a solution in close cooperation with potential users. Other reasons for the use of several different products include a diversity of methods, perhaps at different stages, and a diversity of target systems environments. It may well be possible in time to produce a single CASE tool that can handle the majority of requirements, but such comprehensive products are seldom easy to use.

If we have a variety of products, each performing a valuable task, we need some way of bringing them together. In places the functions may overlap, and there will certainly be a need to share data between them. In particular, for management purposes it will be necessary to collate project control data from all these sources. This sharing of data will not be easy, and may not be possible, unless there is a common approach to the definition and storage of data.

Thirdly, we are considering a growing and changing marketplace, in which new products are constantly being introduced, and existing ones being substantially enhanced. The prudent user will wish to keep his options open, and be free to switch to a new product, or to a new version of an existing product, without difficulty. He would also like some assurance that new products will be able to access existing data.

4   WHAT STANDARDS ARE RELEVANT?

This chapter will concentrate on relevant dictionary standards, and the next section considers these in more detail. However, there are other standards which are relevant, and which the suppliers of CASE tools should follow wherever possible, for their own benefit as much as for the benefit of users.

Much theoretical and practical experience has gone into the development of international database standards, of which there are now two: SQL (relational) and NDL (network). Work continues on SQL, and the level of language now defined goes some way beyond what existing implementations can offer. Incidentally, it is not necessary to refer in this and other contexts to "ANSI SQL"; the work is proceeding in parallel in ANSI and ISO, and many of the enhancements beyond the first standard have come from non-American sources.

Both for their own benefit and for that of users, it would make sense for CASE suppliers to adopt these standards where possible; apart from reducing development effort, this would increase tool portability. The same argument applies to programming languages, for most of which there is an ISO standard, and usually an equivalent ANSI standard.

Within Europe there has been work on a common base for CASE tools, under the ESPRIT programme. Known as the Portable Common Tool Environment (PCTE), this has now been adopted by ECMA (the European Computer Manufacturers' Association) as a potential standard. Again, the major benefit of following the PCTE approach is portability.

Data interchange for CASE is an area in which standards are urgently needed. Work is under way in the USA (EDIF/CASE), and in ISO and ANSI in the context of IRDS. A major concern here is that we will need standards not only for file formats and structures, but also for the types of data which may be transferred; this will require a substantial measure of agreement on working methods and on the contents of the various development deliverables. In this area, as in standards in general, it is regrettable that so few users are able and willing to contribute to standardisation work; in most cases the standards committees are dominated by suppliers and very large (usually government) users.

5 DICTIONARY STANDARDS

During 1984 ANSI proposed the adoption of a work item on Information Resource Dictionary Systems (IRDS) by ISO, and offered its own draft standard as a basis for this work. At meetings in 1985 and 1986 it became clear that other national representatives were not happy with the ANSI approach, and work on an alternative base document was begun. It was initially hoped that the result would be acceptable to ANSI, but this proved not to be the case, and the ANSI document became an ANSI standard in 1988. The major area of concern was the underlying data model, a topic which will recur later; the emphasis on a Command Language and Panel Interface, rather than a software interface for tools, was also considered unsatisfactory.

The UK believes that the current ISO approach will produce a viable family of IRDS standards, and hopes that eventually it will be possible to make these and the ANSI standards converge. Figure 4 illustrates the architecture within which interfaces can be standardised.

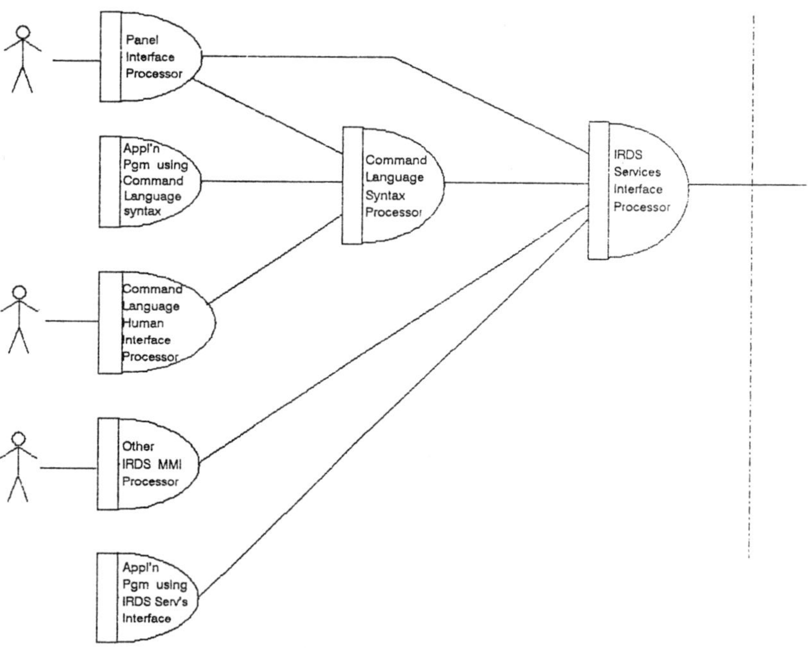

Figure 2.4 : IRDS interfaces.

An IRDS Framework standard, defining this architecture and establishing the framework within which other standards can be defined, has now reached the status of Draft Proposal, and the ballot to raise it to a Draft International Standard closes in September 1989. At the time of writing (March 1989) the IRDS Services Interface is scheduled to go for DP ballot after a meeting in May. Work is also under way on an SQL support standard, defining what a dictionary needs to contain in order to be able to generate SQL database definitions. The problem of data transfer is also receiving attention, in the context both of IRDS and of SQL databases.

The basic principle underlying the ISO work on IRDS is that the IRD should be the standard repository for all data about information and systems, and should be accessible both to software tools and to human users. For this to be possible, the structure of its contents must be extensible both by suppliers and by users. The view has also been taken that existing standards should be used where possible, and SQL has been used in the definition of IRDS data; this does not imply any requirement to implement or access the IRDS using SQL.

A very important principle is that the rules for validating IRD contents must be part of the data definition, so that integrity enforcement can be automatic irrespective of the interface used. This is essential if CASE tools are to be able to depend on the correctness of the data.

As mentioned above, much of the disagreement with ANSI centred on the approach used to model the data contained in the IRD. ISO has adopted an approach based on the relational model, as used in SQL, with a number of extensions giving greater power in expressing constraints; most of these extensions are candidates for addition to the SQL standard, and some have already been included in the latest revision. This approach is in contrast to ANSI's use of a form of Entity-Relationship (E-R) model.

Why does the form of model matter? Basically, the relational model is the result of extensive database experience, both theoretical and practical, and we know it works. Various forms of E-R model have been widely used in analysis, with valuable results, but data definition for an IRD is not just an analysis exercise. When the dictionary administrator defines IRD contents, he is designing a database, and needs the benefits of characteristics such as data independence just like any other database designer. A single example, taken from a situation actually encountered when designing an ANSI-conformant dictionary to support an application generator, will serve to illustrate the problem.

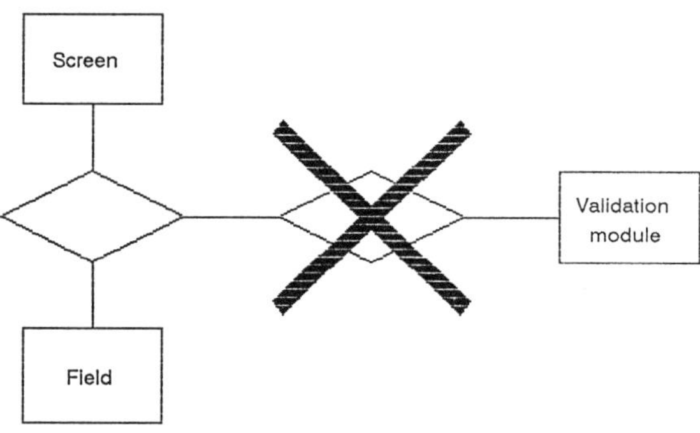

Figure 2.5 : A typical E-R modelling problem.

On the left of Figure 2.5 we have a relationship, represented by a diamond, between screens and fields: each field may appear on many screens, and each screen may contain many fields. Using the E-R approach, this relationship may have attributes, such as the position of the field on the screen. All was well until it was required to associate a validation module with each occurrence of a field on a screen; unfortunately, in common with most E-R models, that chosen by ANSI does not allow relationships to have relationships. In analysis this would not matter; we could just change the model. Here, though, we are specifying a dictionary database, and any subsequent change will be difficult and costly.

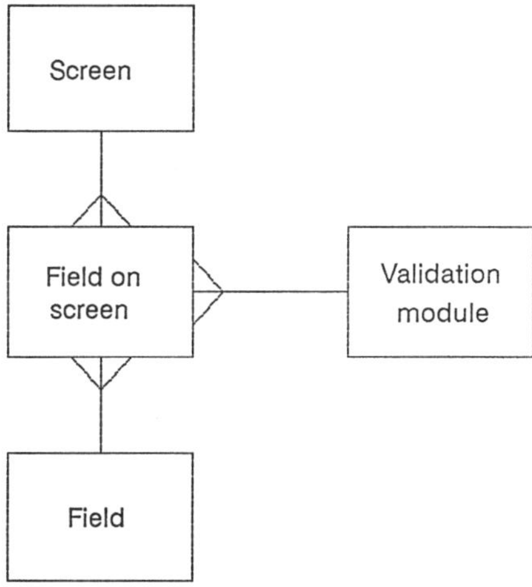

Figure 2.6 : A solution using the ISO IRDS model.

Figure 2.6 shows how the same situation can be represented using the ISO IRDS model, or indeed in SQL. With this approach there is no problem; the second relationship (or association or referential constraint) can be added quite safely even if the dictionary is already populated. To the majority of those involved in the ISO IRDS work, this was an important consideration in providing the necessary flexibility to support CASE tools.

Once the IRDS Services Interface standard is approved, work can continue on extending it to cover all standard programming languages, and perhaps to define a Command Language for human use. Probably more important, though, is work on the definition of the IRD content needed to support common activities. The first of these, on SQL database definition, is well under way. Others may include data analysis and project management, to give just two examples. Reaching agreement on these will not be easy; without it, though, the integration of CASE tools from different suppliers will be impossible.

6   CONCLUSIONS

Without the development and acceptance of standards for data definition, sharing and interchange, CASE technology will never achieve its full potential. We shall be limited to using separate tools for different jobs, with *ad hoc* interfaces between them. Imagine the use of electricity in the home if every room had a different shaped socket, and every appliance a different shaped plug! Users must insist on standards, whether official or *de facto*, if they are to retain control of their own destinies.

3

CCTA AND CASE TECHNOLOGIES REQUIREMENTS FOR SSADM

Brian Strowger
Information Systems Engineering Division
Central Computer and Telecommunications Agency

1 INTRODUCTION

Why is Central Government interested, let alone involved, in this area of development ? With a two billion pound spend every year in purchasing, developing and running systems, using over thirteen thousand people, a competitive, deregulated supply of products and services is imperative.

System developers within government face exactly the same problems as the remainder of the Information Systems world. The nature of many government projects is that they are large systems developed by teams working with end users but working within a framework to structure more carefully the systems development process and its management.

The aim of Information Systems Engineering Division of CCTA is to influence departments to improve productivity and quality and to reduce risk in the management of their information systems. The objective is to provide mechanisms which allow the productivity and quality of the management development, operation and maintenance to improve by 30% by 1990/1991.

The strategy has four main strands.

- Methods. To introduce new and improve current methods which will reduce cost and improve quality.

- Tools to Assist methods. Stimulate the market to supply related tools which improve the productivity and quality of application development and implementation.

- Policy initiatives. Drawing together European, national and departmental initiatives to allow the first and second points above to be taken forward effectively.

- Infrastructure. Help create the European, national, departmental and local initiatives to ensure the first and second points above are effectively progressed.

CCTA's requirement for CASE technologies is a crucial factor for meeting objectives within this programme.

2   METHODS FRAMEWORK

An organisation making the transition to a Software Engineering culture requires a structure which supports corporate planning and business needs. No single method provides a total solution but a methods framework can give broad coverage. This, together with a corporate data policy, should give the basic requirements for CASE.

It also gives problems of integration, consistency, data management communication, completeness, viability, cost, compatibility etc. so the candidate user of CASE will be aiming to populate that framework with tools which provide comprehensive support for the framework's component methods. The tools should help the software engineer to do what needs to be done, not exploit technology for its own sake. The CCTA has a methods framework and is moving to make more of it publicly available, enabling greater use to be made outside as within government.

Looking forward to 1992 and beyond, the European Commission has endorsed the principle of a framework for public procurement and the U.K. is active with the other member states to ensure harmonisation and migration towards a European standard for Software Development.

The CASE environment within a methods framework has two components. A management element which ensures the practitioner and management has the format and understanding which will facilitate the successful utilisation of tools, and an engineering component - the hardware and software technology which makes possible things which were inconceivable a few years ago.

For methods support, the tool cannot be generic, otherwise it becomes like passengers squabbling for deck chairs on the Titanic - fighting for position while the old order collapses beneath them. Without understanding and direction, a good tool just enables the practitioner to build poor, or incorrect, systems faster.

3   SSADM AND CASE

If software engineering is to be robust, then the method itself has to be well defined. If the method is not rich in the concepts needed to form a complete picture, then any computer support tool will be deficient in assisting the practitioner with completeness and consistency checking.

A method which is a tool bag of techniques for representing the various outputs can only be supported by a similar level tool. The method needs an underlying model. Within SSADM, this is achieved by specifying standards.

These standards are :

- Document standards — to define syntax, semantics and information content of each type of document

- Technical standards — to define the method of production and inter-relationships.

- Structural standards — for the sequence of creation and refinement SSADM could be defined as the application of these standards to the analysis and design phase of the waterfall model of the software life cycle.

Computer assistance is feasible and necessary. Introduction of rigorous methods impose development overheads, tools provide the productivity. Many approaches are offered, from PC drawing tools, through workstations to mainframe based product sets. Often technical sophistication lacks integration and interoperability with variable support for methods and many methods on offer. To put a focus in the market place the DTI and CCTA have employed the SSADM research centre to provide an SSADM tool conformance scheme. The aim is to make it easier for buyers to buy and sellers to sell. Jeet Khaira will detail this.

The full requirement is for a breadth of support for SSADM support tools, extended to provide CASE facilities for business analysis at the front end and a variety of implementation processes at the other - 3GL and 4GL code within a PM/CM framework. Breadth alone is not enough, the requirement is for depth of support as well, something beyond a simple graphics drawing tool and word processor package.

There is need for support for the structural standards to give guidance and enforcing sequence, ensuring completeness. Documentation standards of syntax for notation and semantics of information content, identifying sources and re-use in other documents. Technical standards to prescribe the detailed activities to be undertaken. These can all be integrated in tools, covering function, information and time, giving error specification and explanation. Usability on presentation are important elements in ensuring the tool practitioner can use and understand the product set he or she is expected to use. None of this is, or was, achieved overnight.

At the beginning of the decade there was a need to prove that SSADM support tools could be built and CCTA undertook significant prototyping work to prove the feasibility, using multi-user PC workstations. New technology advances were tried as they emerged, became stable and were applicable. Some were discarded, such as the use of transputers as screen support devices, others were taken up and included - use of GEM windows as a MMI environment. Wherever possible suppliers were encouraged to take advantage of this work to get products to users and the role is now changing to make the models and specifications available to tool vendors, work even more closely with users and provide evaluation of products.

The current approach is to review the market place, find means of helping to ensure full coverage and ensure that as SSADM evolves, it becomes even easier to "software-ise". The *de facto* standard of SSADM in itself has created a significant market place and we wish to ensure a deregulated supply of quality tools available to the public sector with external support of consultancy, training and complementary methods and tools. There is a need to move towards standards for data sorage and exchange (PCTE, IRDS, EDIF, CDIF...), standards for HCI (Presentation Manager, GEM, Motif, X/Windows...), standards for operating systems (OS-2, DOS, Unix, AIX..) etc.

4   SSADM AND CASE — THE TECHNOLOGY REQUIREMENT

The current CCTA approach to methods development is to acquire a bespoke methods development workbench and toolwriters toolkit for the production of methods support tools, using SSADM as the first model.

The concept is to provide support for all stages of a structured method, with complete checking of information across the project yet still permitting a team, or teams, of people to work on a project sharing information but not impacting on each other. The objectives are to address practitioner issues by providing multi-user, multi-window environment with high power graphic workstations, give method support for the documents, steps, stages and tasks of SSADM; encapsulate expertise in the tools; build in configuration management and be supplied in an inherently flexible and extensible architecture with maximum portability.

For SSADM this means coverage of the complete method, integration of different kinds of information, rule enforcement, configuration and project management, support for team working and exploitation of advanced hardware.

The overall architecture is quite simple. The native environment and operating system - SUN O/S - provide file storage, system utilities and network and process management. Above this is a kernel containing document management, graphics components, processing components and user management. This layer is designed and written for system portability. The next layer is the infrastructure of task management functions, document creation, presentation and amendment, plus the deliverable management functions. The infrastructure provides extensibility - new objects or elements are added to meet the requirements of any given method. Finally the methods toolset, in this version, the SSADM toolset for the structural, technical and procedural standards of SSADM.

The methods workbench architecture consists of two parts. An infrastructure, which contains the elements needed for a method, and a collection of tasks and documents which are method specific.

For this, the technology requirements are simple. Large screens, full graphics, maximum processing power, security/integrity, portability, adherence to relevant standards and an object management system. All readily available now.

5   SSADM AND CASE — THE USER REQUIREMENT

A CASE product has to be multi-user for organisation-wide team working. This means good data management to ensure that shared information is consistent, complete and to quality while allowing individuals to work on draft documents until they are presented and found acceptable for wider access. In this way a team of practitioners working independently of each other work with controlled copies of the central information. Their individual work is also made available to others when it is suitable to be used.

Project management becomes a key factor. Not the progress of work against planned progress, but the definition of the project in terms of documents and SSADM tasks, with the allocation of these tasks to a practitioner.

Method support is paramount, both in coverage and following standards. SSADM has a number of stages, each with a series of steps and collection of tasks to produce one or more documents such as dataflow diagrams, logical data structures, entity life histories, entity function descriptions, blank narrative text etc. The standards are supported by rules which help the practitioner construct the correct model. These are at varying levels of complexity from simple rules for individual objects, the more complex intra-document rules covering structure, inter-document rules for items such as elements on a dataflow diagram to catalogues and process descriptions and finally rules which control the way work is done — the addition of "expertise".

However the line between expertise for user support and a rigid toolset which does not recognise the inherent flexibility of SSADM can be a fine one.

6   CCTA METHODS WORKBENCH

This has been acquired by CCTA to model and develop methods. The infrastructure is method independent and contains a number of predefined general classes and services which would be common to all methods. These can be extended for specific methods.

The infrastructure was specified and written in Z to describe the operations available to managers, practitioners and method toolwriters. The common services cannot be modified by the toolwriters but the general classes can be extended and specialised to produce method-specific deliverables and tasks.

The general classes support diagrams, tables, matrices and tasks etc. These are then specialised for a particular method.

For SSADM the common services include:

- project management for the definition of documents, the tasks needed to produce them and the allocation of those tasks to practitioners,

- configuration management for version control, the release of documents to practitioners and the status of documents,

- allocation of machine resources, machine configuration and network communication, and

- back up and recovery facilities at both the individual machine and project machine level.

The specialist classes for SSADM are of three types.

6.1 Document classes

Each SSADM document is defined according to its individual characteristics, and has two sets of rules.

- Intra-document rules to ensure consistency within the document, that the syntax is correct. For example all entities in a logical data structure have names and relationships are drawn correctly.

- Inter-document rules for consistency between documents and hence the system model itself. For example each entity in a LDS appears in the entity description table and there are no duplicates.

6.2 View classes

These present the documents on the screen , acting as the Man Machine Interface for dialogue between the practitioner and the model of the document currently being created or updated.

6.3 Task classes

These control the allocation of work to practitioners, the order in which SSADM tasks are performed, the automatic transfer of entries to related documents and control the invocation and execution of rules. They are constructed to reflect good practise and provide embedded expertise.

6.4 Method model

Construction of such a method model could be an extensive task, there being 275 documents and associated tasks within version 3 of SSADM. An object-orientated approach and implementation language has reduced this effort. The re-use of common definitions between different document types and the inheritance within classes reduce both programming and testing effort.

The resulting toolset ensures that at any stage of an SSADM project there is a coherent picture of the state of the project as a system model. This model being analagous to a central data dictionary.

Project management is based on the concept of a central project machine controlling a network of individual machines supporting practitioners. Work and resources are allocated to a practitioner, who returns his production to the central function when it is ready for Quality Assurance. No information, once committed by the practitioner, is ever discarded. Configuration management takes care of each version when a document is created or updated. Once a new version is available, this is made known to anyone who needs to be aware and transferred to the task.

7   FURTHER ADVANTAGES

The object-orientated approach also allows each SSADM document to be treated as an object in its own right, with its own structure, behaviour and rules. Thus the toolwriter can define these objects and methods of interaction with the practitioner, or other objects, to extend or modify the toolset or to integrate/interface with other products or tools.

Although the methods workbench can be expanded to support other methods, this is not a light task. The technology of the infrastructure is no problem, it is onerous work of specifying the method itself. To produce a detailed specification in terms of model and view objects, the rules, help text and tasks. The less rigour and structure in the method then the more difficult the task.

Extension and flexibility to method support are key requirements of the workbench. A method needs to evolve and extend to reflect practitioner needs, recognise that a project may use only a subset of the method, and that practitioners will have differing skill levels in use of the method. The toolset must be able to reflect this. To evolve and be be adaptable if it is not to cause frustration, become a straitjacket or otherwise impede its users.

8 SUMMARY

CASE is progressing. Over 1.9 million people in the European community are involved in the labour intensive production of application software. The CASE market world wide is estimated at #400 million and the products are developing rapidly. Without the emergence of clear cut standards and direction, the market is very diversified. There are risks to vendors investing in R and D which will never see a return, and to buyers who could be locked in to expensive and extensive investments in products where direction is not visible or open to influence. Hidden costs of take-up include the price of internal support, external training for tools and methods, losses from the mis- directed or non-coordinated effort of CASE users etc.

CASE tools have become strategic investments. Not necessarily mega size expenditure on a multi-terminal clustered network of a commercial IPSE but an investment in the management of change and the work environment as well as the technology itself. Organisations and projects operate in differing cultural, budgetary and technical environments. No single or simple CASE tool can cope with all of that but ANY open, non-proprietary approach will work IF it is used in a controlled and directed way. It is more likely that successes claimed for methods and tools are due, in significant part, to good management and control, rather than the perfection of the development procedures and processes used.

4
CASE AND PROTOTYPING

Darrel Ince
Dept of Computing, Faculty of Mathematics, Open University,
Milton Keynes, MK7 6AA

1   INTRODUCTION

Requirements analyis is one of the most difficult tasks that occur during the software project. There are a number of reasons for this: the cultural difference between customers and developers, the nature of the documentation generated during the analysis process and the size of the documentation. Prototyping: the development of a model of a proposed system, has been a successful attempt to overcome these problems. However, the success of prototyping leads to problems.

These problems arise from the success of the prototyping process: as developers are finding that prototyping is a major aid in requirements analysis, they are becoming more and more ambitious in the size and complexity of the systems that they attempt to prototype. This leads to major problems in communication. For example, it can be very difficult even after a break of a day or two to discover what the functions of the current prototype are, and with a prototype being developed by a team there are the same problems in communication that occur in large conventional projects. Before looking at some of the solutions to these problems it is worth describing the three main modes of prototyping (Hekm 86).

Throw-away prototyping consists of developing a quick and dirty version of a software system, and then carrying out a cyclical process of evaluation and modification, until the customer is happy with the prototype that has been developed. The prototype is then frozen and conventional software development begins.

Incremental prototyping involves the developer partitioning user requirements into subsets of non-overlapping functions. For example, a system for monitoring and controlling a chemical plant might be partitioned into sets of functions for monitoring pressure and temperature, for controlling the plant by means of actuating valves or regulating chemical flow, for displaying results to plant operators, and providing a database of information which enables engineers to run the plant economically. Incremental prototyping involves the delivery of a system in planned stages where each stage implements one of the non- overlapping subsets of functionality (Floy 1984). The advantage of incremental prototyping is that it enables the developer to split up a main project into a series of mini-projects, each of which should have a higher esprit-de-corps, and do not possess the communicational complexity of large projects. The last point is important: by splitting up a project into mini-projects, the manager minimises the amount of interaction between staff and enables a much higher proportion of staff time to be spent on developmental activities (Broo 87).

The reason that we class this form of development as prototyping is that it allows the developer to choose, as his first delivery, that part of the system which has the most fuzzy requirements. While it is true that not all systems contain clean non-overlapping functional subsets, some of which have fuzzy requirements and some of which do not, there is a significant number that possess this property and, hence, allow us to call the production of early versions of a system with limited functionality a form of prototyping.

Evolutionary prototyping is an attempt to take into account change in a software system. There are two ways of looking at a software project. The first, borrowed from a model used in other engineering disciplines, envisages the development of a software system as a series of phased activities: requirements analysis, system specification, system design, detailed design and programming, with the end-product from one phase for example, the system design being regarded as the input into the next phase.

This model of software development regards the software project as being relatively strictly delineated, although, to be fair to its proponents, they do point out that a limited degree of feedback does occur in many projects: for example an error, committed during system design, which is only detected during implementation, will require system design to be carried out during the implementation phase.

Evolutionary prototyping is in complete antithesis to this model as it regards software development certainly of medium to large projects as being an evolutionary activity, where, if you take a time slice through a software project, a large number of separate activities will occur (McCr 1982).

The reason for this seemingly radical view of software development is change. One aspect of this change has already been touched upon: the need for re-working to occur when an error committed during one phase is discovered during a subsequent phase. However, there is a more serious reason for change: the dynamic nature of user requirements. The world is a rapidly changing place: business strategy changes, mergers occur, new defence technology is introduced, new laws are instigated and new reporting procedures are invented. Such changes give rise to new or modified requirements which have to be taken into account in software which interacts with the world.

The nature of such change is clearly seen during software maintenance, where requirements changes form the major proportion of modifications after a system has been placed in operation (Lien 80). However, requirements changes often impinge on software projects during development; especially if they are medium to large projects which occupy a substantial time-scale.

The developer who experiences change during the execution of a software project has two options. The first is to insist that he will develop the software that has been contracted for, according to the system specification. Since the vast majority of software contracts specify the system specification as the base document of the software project a document which all subsequent developmental activities depend the developer has every right to do this. However, the wise software developer attempts to take a second option.

This option involves incorporating change in the software product during development. There are a number of pre- conditions for this strategy to work: first, the developer requires a good configuration control system, preferably one that is automated. Second, he should have established a proper procedure for agreeing change and costing the effect of change. Third he should adopt strategies, such as information hiding (Parn 72), which enable change to be tolerated by a system architecture. The developer who takes this course acknowledges change as a fact of life, and assumes that it is a better strategy to meet a high proportion of real requirements, rather than a set of requirements enshrined and frozen in this system specification many of which are out of date.

Evolutionary prototyping is an improvement over throw- away prototyping in that software development is based on a prototype which always remains executable during the software project. What happens during evolutionary prototyping is that during development the original prototype is gradually refined and made more efficient, and is also modified in response to changes in user requirements, any changes which are required during the project can be exhibited by the developer in the current version of the prototype.

Evolutionary prototyping is at variance with both throw- away prototyping and incremental prototyping, in that a phase- oriented software development model cannot be used. At this stage it is worth pointing out there are major management problems in controlling a project with such a high degree of dynamics.

2   THE SOLUTION

Given the three modes of prototyping described above how can the problem of communication in prototyping be solved. The answer is conceptually simple; however, implementing it, in practice, is difficult, although a number of software tools are emerging which enable the communication problem to be solved. The solution is to ensure that the specification of a system is kept in step with the prototype. If this was so, the development team would no longer have to read the text of a 4GL, look at UNIX shell code, or examine the source code of a very high level language in order to communicate internally in a prototyping project.

Now, there are problems in following this advice, the major one is that it can be a highly resource-intensive process keeping the specification in step with the prototype, especially since the nature of prototyping is such that much work will be discarded. Even with the support of some analyst workbenches that have diagramming facilities, many developers would reject this suggestion, even if it was pointed out that the specification would need to be developed anyway. However, there are some promising solutions to this dilemma.

2.1 The wide-spectrum language

This sub-section describes a particular system, partly developed by the author, which was constructed with evolutionary prototyping in mind. The system is based on a wide-spectrum language EPROL. Such a language consists of facilities which enable the developer to specify, design and implement a system and which is executable at all times during the software project.

EPROL also contains extensive facilities for the human computer interface: forms, dialogues and pop-up menus. Full details of these can be found in (Ince 87). Since EPROL is a wide- spectrum language, it is capable of being used as a medium for evolutionary prototyping. For example, a system being developed can partly exist as a functional specification, partly as a design and partly as an implementation. Even though the system is in such a mixed form it is capable of being prototyped, thus satisfying the requirements for an evolutionary prototyping medium.

Evolutionary development in EPROS consists of specification followed by design and implementation until the system is expressed purely in terms of implementation facilities. The final prototype can then be easily translated into a conventional programming language such as C or Pascal.

It is also possible to use EPROL as a throw-away prototyping medium in that a system can be specified using the functional specification facilities of the language, and then evaluated and modified, until the user and the developer are happy with the result. The important point about such a solution is that the executable version of the system, which for much of the time will exist as a specification, will be able to be read relatively easily by staff who carry out the prototyping.

The only disadvantage in this approach is that the specification and design notation used in EPROL is mathematical a notation which many software developers find difficulty with. However, the imminent publication of defence standard 00-55 should mean that, in a relatively short time, in the safety critical defence software area, there will be a pool of expertise.

2.2 Fifth-generation languages

A second solution involves fifth-generation or functional programming languages. These languages have arisen in response to two problems with conventional programming languages, such as Pascal and Ada. The first problem is that conventional programming languages are ill-matched for the multi-processor systems that VLSI technology is making possible. Programs written in conventional languages, and run on such computers, tend to spend a large proportion of their time communicating and synchronising, this leads to less time spent in useful work. The second problem is that conventional languages tend to have messy semantics and this leads to difficulties in proving that systems meet their specification (Back 78). Functional languages have clean semantics and programs expressed in such languages are capable of being reasoned about much more easily than languages such as Pascal.

Functional languages such as ML (Wiks 87) and Miranda (Turn 85) are capable of expressing the types of specification and design described in the previous sub-section, in a very similar way to EPROL. Although these languages do not contain the conventional programming facilities found in EPROL, advances in new hardware architectures over the next five years should enable the execution of designs to be as efficient as the execution of the implementation facilities of EPROL.

Another medium which can be used in an evolutionary way is SETL (Schw 86). This is a very high level language which has data types based on mathematical sets and, hence, can be used to describe systems using methods such as VDM. Moreover, SETL contains a data representation sub-language which allows the developer to fine tune the data structures used in SETL for efficiency. Thus, a developer who uses SETL could write functional specifications, such as those outlined in section 3, and then gradually refine these specifications by fine-tuning the underlying data representation. A description of SETL used to prototype an Ada compiler can be found in (Kruc 84).

2.3 Prolog

Prolog has gained attention because of its use in artificial intelligence applications. However, it is also a good medium for prototyping. Prolog programs consist of a series of statements known as a Horn clause. They specify that if a series of conditions are true then a particular result will occur. The general form of a Horn clause is

condition1, condition2, ..., conditionn − > action

and this matches the natural structure of many specifications, for example, that for a reactor monitoring system might contain statements such as

> if the reactor is in monitor mode, and the main inlet valve is open, and an abnormal rise in temperature is detected then an alarm signal is emitted.

It is relatively easy to translate statements such as the one above to Prolog, and then execute the resulting program as a prototype.

2.4 Executable data flow diagrams

It has been pointed outmost notably in (Dock 86)that the data flow diagrams employed in most structured methodologies are capable of being executed. That it should be possible for the user of an analyst workbench to step his way through a data flow diagram stored in some internal form.

Research in this area is still in its early days. For example, it is still problematical what the relationship of a data dictionary is to an executable data flow diagram prototype. However, we are beginning to see some quite impressive systems which allow early prototypes to be developed and linked up with the HCI generating parts of a CASE workbench. Probably the most impressive is the Prokit Workbench marketed by McDonnel Douglas Information Systems.

3   SUMMARY

The solutions outlined in the previous section represent the first step towards providing a facility for prototyping within the distributed CASE environment. Each has its own advantages and disadvantages. The advantage of the wide-spectrum approach is that it can be used for all types of prototyping but it is confined to mathematical notations. The advantage of fifth-generation languages is that many of the languages are commercially available, but that such languages can only be used for throw- away prototyping and are rather mathematical. The advantage of Prolog is that it is commercially available, many versions of the language can interface with HCI facilities, but that it can only be used for throw-away prototyping. The advantage of excutable data flow diagrams is that it corresponds to industrial practice but is only confined to throw-away prototyping.

4   REFERENCES

(Back 78) J. Backus. Can programming be liberated from the von Neumann style? A functional style and its algebra of programs. Communications of the ACM. 21, 8. 613641. 1978.

(Broo 87) F.P. Brookes Jr. No silver bullet, essence and accidents of software engineering. IEEE Computer. April. 1018. 1987.

(Dock 86)T.W.G. Docker and G. Tate. Executable data flow diagrams. Proc. Software Engineering 86. 352370. 1986.

(Floy 84) C. Floyd. A systematic look at prototyping. In Approaches to Prototyping. Berlin:Springer-Verlag. 118. 1984..

(Hekm 86) S. Hekmatpour and D. Ince. Rapid Software Prototyping. Oxford Surveys in Information Technology. 3. 3776. 1986.

(Ince 87) D. Ince and S. Hekmatpour. Evolutionary Prototyping and the humancomputer interface. Proceedings Interact 87. 479 484. 1987.

(Kruc 84) P. Kruchten and E. Schonberg. The Ada/Ed system: a large scale experiment in software prototyping using SETL. In Approaches to Prototyping. Berlin:Springer-Verlag. 398415. 1984..

(Lien 80) B.P. Lientz and E.B. Swanson. Software Maintenance Management. Reading, MA:Addison-Wesley. 1980.

(McCr 82) D.D. McCracken and M.A. Jackson. Life cycle concept considered harmful. ACM SIGSOFT Software Engineering Notes. 7, 2. 2932. 1982.

(Parn 72) D.L. Parnas. On the criteria to be used for decomposing systems into modules. Communications ACM. 15, 12. 10531058. 1972.

(Schw 86) J.T. Schwartz, R.B.K. Dewar, E. Dubinsky and E. Schonberg. Programming with Sets. An Introduction to SETL. New York, NY: Springer-Verlag. 1986.

(Turn 85) D. Turner. Functional programs as executable specifications. In Mathematical Logic and Programming Languages. London:Prentice-Hall. 1985.

(Wiks 87) A. Wikstrom. Functional Programming Using Standard ML. London: Prentice-Hall. 1987.

5

CASE AND METHODOLOGIES

Geoffrey Rose
SCOLL

1   INTRODUCTION

Methodologies have matured since they were introduced in the early 1970s to cope with the complexities of database file design. Diagrammatic techniques, based on general systems theory, were interfaced to bring progressively more analysis and design aspects of computer systems into the methodology. The use of CAD programmes to help maintain the technique diagrams, lead rapidly to the desire to hold supporting analytical information in an integrated manner within the same PC. The CASE Analyst Workbench which resulted from this need, became possible only when the PCs became powerful enough to support a data dictionary in which the analyst information could be held. Design of the data dictionary, entailed the usage of the data modelling technique from within the methodology. This paper looks at the way in which the use of a methodology to design its own support tools, has resulted in the flexible CASE tools which will be an integral part of system implementation in the 1990s.

2   METHODOLOGIES - CURRENT POSITION

2.1 Purpose

Over the past three years, the computer press has spent many column inches on discussing the merits of one methodology against another. Tom Gilb[1] is very clear in his message that the purpose of any product must be defined openly, together with a set of measurable attributes, before the product's worth can be discussed. A methodology's purpose is defined in three parts. The purpose of a methodology is to ensure;

- delivered software systems are of the required quality

- the delivered quality is measurable

- the quality of the deliverable system is predictable

As soon as this is understood, it ceases to be meaningful to discuss whether one methodology is better than another or whether a prototyping methodology should be adopted by a modern systems development manager in preference to one encompassing a rigorous systems engineering approach. The Systems Development Manager's task is to match the quality of systems required with the quality that a methodology is designed to deliver. A mis-match in quality between the required systems and the employed methodology, produces under or over engineered software. In either case the DP department will bear the cost.

2.2 Methodology attributes

Three major attributes for any product are

- usability

- performance

- adaptability

Any DP manager setting out to install a methodology needs to subdivide the major attributes into a hierarchy of measurable qualities.

The usability of a methodology would be an aggregate value of the methodology's comprehensiveness, comprehensibility, its ability to motivate development staff into using it and its helpfulness to those half way through the learning curve.

The comprehensiveness of a methodology is determined by the complexity and quality of the systems to be developed. Gilb would argue that this is sufficient comprehensiveness.

Another of Gilb's major concepts is that of the open system architecture. This endows a methodology with the quality of adaptability which allows the methodology to develop in line with the changing needs of an organisation's application profile.

Regardless of the quality issue, every methodology must deliver enhanced performance on the development staff. Several qualities give rise to enhanced performance. The major quality claimed by methodologies, is that the developers data capture is formalised. The methodology's selected task is to ensure that redundant data isn't captured unnecessarily giving rise to high documentation maintenance costs as a result of data inconsistency.

The standard approaches of a methodology should provide a repeat for results for each development task. This opens the way to increased performance in the testing of quality, as each member of staff involved in testing should have the same view of correctness.

2.3 Technique orientation

Major dominant methodologies have their origins in the late 1970s/early 1980s. Based on good software engineering principles, Yourdon and Jackson developed different diagrammatic techniques to help program designers structure programs of high quality. As the quality of program design and construction improves through the use of these techniques, it became clear that many of the system design faults lay in the approach to analysis and design. This prompted Yourdon, Jackson and BIS amongst others to identify diagrammatic techniques which would aid the analyst and systems designer. Today's major methodologies still bear this pedigree.

They consist of a task list, a set of deliverables based firmly on the techniques used to produce them and the techniques themselves. This technique orientation for the production of methodologies, has led to problems in the translation of one deliverable to another in the different stages of a systems development cycle. Work done by James Martin, to support the design of Information Engineering Facility, has helped identify the underlying conceptual data models for the development cycle. For methodologies to develop beyond their technique orientation, methodology designers need a clear understanding of the concepts underlying each system's development stage.

2.4 Strategic considerations

As with any product, consultancies marketing implementations of a methodology, need mechanisms to differentiate their product from others available. Methodologies consist of

- task lists grouped into development stages,

- a set of deliverables to be produced by the tasks,

- techniques designed to allow the tasks to be performed.

These four attributes, tasks, techniques, deliverables and development stage in combination provide considerable scope for product differentiation to enable the client base, once established, to be protected.

Methodologies have chosen to use graphical techniques to exploit the diagram's ability to display information rigorously and succinctly. The number and types of diagram available to perform the different tasks are limited. Differentiation between products, therefore, has had to concentrate more on the presentation of the diagrams in terms of the shape of the symbols and the amount of information that each diagram type is required to store. In several instances, this need to demonstrate product differentiation which has led some methodology designers to lose sight of software engineering principles and to produce diagram types which are difficult to maintain. Dataflow diagrams fall into this category where, coupled into a single diagram, are views of function, data, events and, very often, functional dependency.

Diagram types have been used for different conceptual purposes. In LSDM/SSADM the data model, called the logical data structure, is viewed mainly as a vehicle for determining the database design which will support the application software. In information engineering the conceptual data model is seen very much more as a business analysis tool. These two different concepts of purpose lead to a different style of data model.

The different concepts behind methodology design have lead not only to differentiation in the style of the diagrams but also in the functional scope of the whole methodology. Information engineering's business perspective has allowed the use of techniques to spread up into the functional area of information system strategy planning. LBMS introduced the LEAP methodology to cover information systems strategy planning whilst CCTA have defined a generic approach to strategy studies only requiring the output from any strategy study to be compatible with the SSADM interface. The differences in functional scope is even more marked when one looks at the older methodologies such as MASCOT which starts with logical function design.

The major perceived similarity between the methodologies is that they all assume the green fields start. Many DP managers are wary of adopting a methodology because they have vast investment in existing software. This makes the adoption of methodologies perceived to have green fields starts to be unattractive. Analysis of the current system advocated by Gane & Sarson and any other methodologies incorporating their approach, ought to overcome this reservation but none of the CASE study examples starts with anything other than the manual system.

3   CASE TOOLS - CURRENT POSITION

3.1 Purpose

Early users of methodologies recognised quickly that the maintenance of diagrams was consuming considerable amounts of project development effort. This was compounded by the human inability to maintain consistency across several sets of diagrams which are generated over an elapsed period of time of several weeks.

The first requirement for alternated aid, was to ease the maintenance of the required quality of the deliverables, specifically to aid the checking of consistency both within a diagram and across the set of diagrams. The ability to check consistency required the tool designer to build in an understanding of the consistency rules of any technique. This leads fairly naturally to the development of rules for converting one diagram type produced in one development stage into another diagram type produced in a subsequent stage with an understanding of these conversion rules it is possible conceptually, to place the task of conversion on the tool. If the analyst has specified the system requirements correctly, the tools should be capable of converting these requirements to software systems of a required quality.

Although we are not at the stage of having a fully working and a reliable integrated project support environment tool, the aim of many tool designers is to aid the systems developers to deliver software systems of guaranteed quality.

3.2 CASE tool attributes

For CASE tools to be used successfully in support of a methodology they must possess the required quality attributes of usability, performance and adaptability.

Usability requires the tool to be compatible with the methodology diagrammatic techniques and to hold the data necessary to create the methodology deliverables. The need to differentiate between methodologies has forced the CASE tool market down two different routes. The first, illustrated by tools like IEW and CCTA's MUST is designed to support one methodology specifically. Other vendors have attempted to build a CASE tool which supports several different methodologies providing alternative diagram types but which leaves integration of the deliverables to the analyst, as with Excelerator.

Usability also requires the tool to be compatible with the information technology environment. This includes the data dictionary, the mainframe, and any other productivity enhancing tools such as fourth-generation languages. Again tools are forced into two camps, either to choose a specific information technology environment, illustrated by tools running on IBM mainframes such as IEF, or to make the tool a PC application with compatibility reduced to the level of exporting ASCII flat files.

Besides recording analytical and design data, the systems developer needs to present integrated deliverables. The text manipulating power of word processing packages needs to be available to the developer for the production of reports. Excelerator provides this facility by incorporating limited wordprocessing capability which produces text files compatible with the diagram files. Excelerator and Hoskyns design aid have both chosen to provide wordprocessing facilities within the tool. These allow the developer to cut and paste text and diagrams into a presentation report. Other tools such as IEW have chosen to provide Wordprocessing facilities by basing wordprocessing compatibility at the file level in particular IEW is compatible with any wordprocessing and desk-top publishing package which can handle GEM files.

Integration of an individual developer's text and diagrammatic products, needs to be extended to integration of products from all members of a development team. MUST was designed to provide product integration for projects of four concurrent developers but for the majority of PC based CASE tools multi-user support depends upon project planning to split projects into discrete functional areas and for human skill to sort out differences in areas of overlap.

For project teams to adopt a CASE tool, it must provide an improvement on manual performance. Capturing diagrammatic data initially on a PC for the majority of development staff is a labour-intensive activity. Currently, performance improvement comes from the ability of CASE tools to check for consistency and to limit the impact of change to the area in which the change is required.

Additional performance can be gained by the intelligent capture of data. This permits the developer to enter the data once, preferably on a diagram, and this data to then be re-used and displayed on every other diagram where the data should appear. IEW illustrates this with its totally integrated view of the processes in a functional decomposition chart and in the equivalent of dataflow diagrams.

The layout of diagrams can greatly influence the comprehension of the data they seek to display. A great deal of the initial diagram drawing time is spent trying to achieve a layout in a form from which the presented information is easy to assimilate. Great productivity gains could be made using tools with intelligent graphics capabilities. These would enable the development staff to record the graphical data rapidly leaving the tool to re-arrange the diagram with maximum clarity. IEW and IEF both provide an automatic redraw facility but do not cope adequately with diagrams that are recorded with no thought applied to the layout.

The fourth aspect of performance improvement would come from the automation of data conversion from one development stage to the next. The ideal is the automatic production of code from detailed functional requirements. IEF, IEW and Corevision have all made steps along this road but from press reports, it still seems that practical application of this conversion for anything other than comparatively simple functions is still some way off.

Adaptability, the third required attribute, recognises that methodologies are not static. SSADM has a planned and published development programme, Yourdon adopted the Ward and Mellor editions for real time systems, MASCOT has developed an interface to SSADM all of which is illustrative of methodologies adapting to cope with new requirements. CASE tools need to be adaptable in order to provide continuing support for the changing methodologies. Excelerator, VSF and others provide configurable graphics which enable the symbols on diagrams to be tailored to provide support for the methodologies particular implementation of a technique. VSF has taken adaptability a stage further by making the rules for the methodology configurable. This permits development staff to change the techniques or indeed the methodology to produce the equivalent deliverable data in a more efficient way.

3.3 Development stage orientation

The functional scope of different types of CASE tools illustrates the historical development of CASE tools to support the changing needs of the data processing departments. The CASE tool market has grown bottom up, initially to support the labour-intensive stages of detailed software design and construction. This group of product types, now termed the Lower CASE tools includes the programmers IPSE, such as Philips MAESTRO, fourth-generation languages, application generators and the DBMS products which were the initiators of the CASE tool and methodology market.

A decade passed between IBM's database product IMS and the introduction of the first analyst workbench. Analyst workbenches are designed to support the detailed requirements study and some of the analytical tasks of tactical studies. This left a gap between the functional specification resulting from the detailed requirements study and the detailed specifications required as input for the Lower CASE tools. This has been filled partially by the design workbench but because of the environment sensitive nature of design, there is still a need for products which have complete and rigorous interfaces to the code producing Lower CASE tools.

CCTA is encouraging, although not funding, Lower CASE tool vendors to put design effort into defining the interface between their product and SSADM. The results of this work should greatly aid the development of what looks like the philosophers stone of the DP world, the integrated project support environment tool. IEF is the most successful of the IPSE type of tool but as stated previously, the success is limited. Today's development effort is directed more towards the production of discrete but integrated CASE tools, I-CASE. The modular approach of I-CASE will be adaptable to different technical environments and the changing needs of the development staff within the different life-cycle changes. Hoskyns have taken this approach with their life-cycle products which attempt to integrate their project management tool, PMW, with their development tool, Design Aid.

Strategy studies which head up the systems development cycle are supported by only a few products such as Knowledgeware's Planning Workbench, largely because the market is still seen as a small one and the scope for productivity improvement for automation is limited. The major strength of planning workbenches is the provision of versatile matrix manipulation. The matrix is a valuable technique, frequently required in analysis. The current analyst workbenches would be enhanced significantly if matrix support were included.

3.4 Strategic market considerations

The CASE tool market is large and highly competitive. The pie chart of Figure 5.1 illustrates the number of competitive products addressing the additional functional stages of the development cycle. Vendors need to find ways of differentiating their products in order to build their own client base.

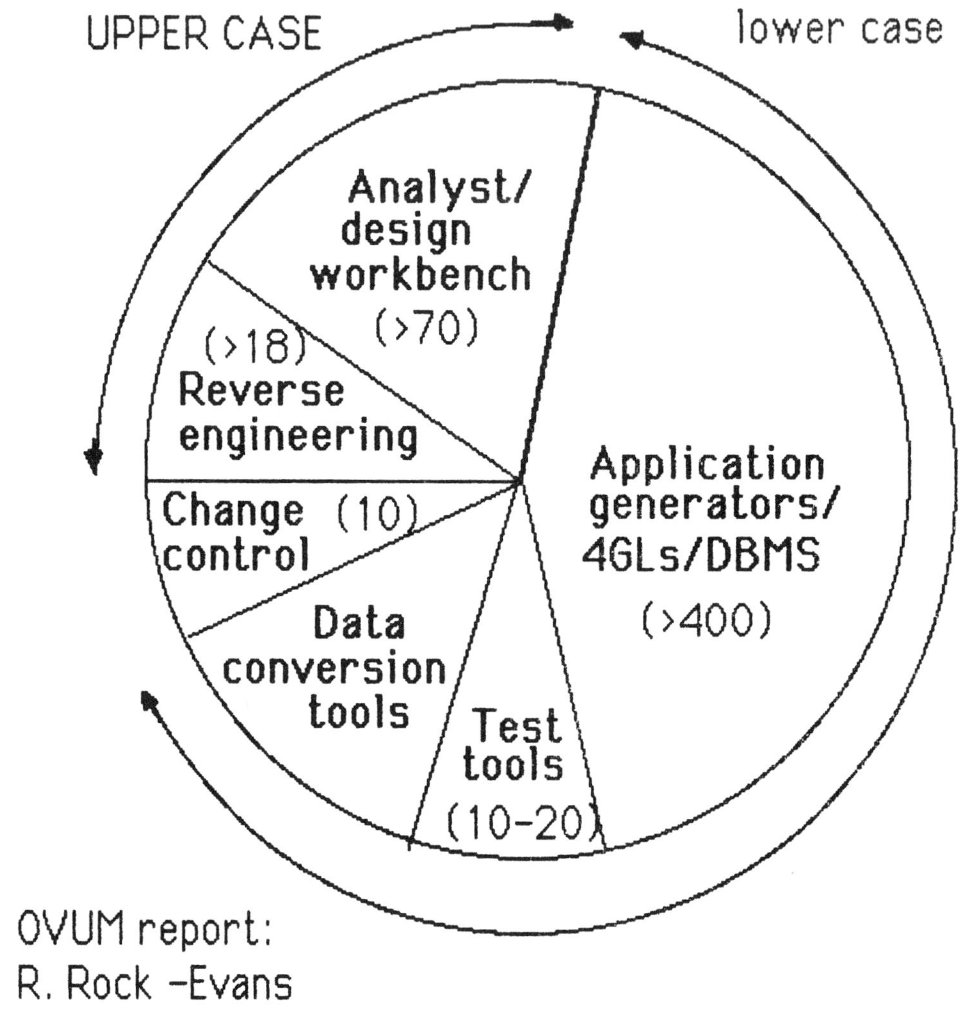

Figure 5.1 : The market position.

The most natural differentiation is the tailoring of the product to support a particular methodology. This results in the workbench tools supporting a specific set of techniques and graphical symbol shapes. This serves to build a client base for both the CASE tool vendor and the methodology vendor. The most successful example is Arthur Young's marketing of IEW where the introduction of the CASE tool has in many instances resulted in the introduction of information engineering to enable IEW to be used successfully. For Lower CASE tools, design workbenches and programmer productivity tools, differentiation is based on the host software environment with the majority targeted on IBM products. All the products are marketed on the promise of improved productivity. For analyst workbenches, this is based on the ability to perform consistency checking and to provide comprehensive diagram editing facilities.

The promise of productivity gains from automatic data conversion from one stage to another awaits the successful introduction of the I-CASE tool set.

4 THE WAY FORWARD

4.1 SDC - conceptual models

Methodologies have been used to analyse themselves. This approach was taken initially to identify the structure of the data dictionaries incorporated within the CASE tool. These meta models were based on the techniques incorporated within a methodology and mixed the underlying conceptual model of the business with the physical model of the technique. TW Olle[2] and others have separated out the conceptual business models. These models at detailed analysis stage contain the major objects which model the external behaviour of the business, the activities of the business area under study and the information that the activities require. The model in Figure 5.2 illustrates that the relationships between these objects and the whole model is technique independent. The designer's task is to translate the entities of the analysis stage into the design entities. The major objects of the design stage, are function and data group.

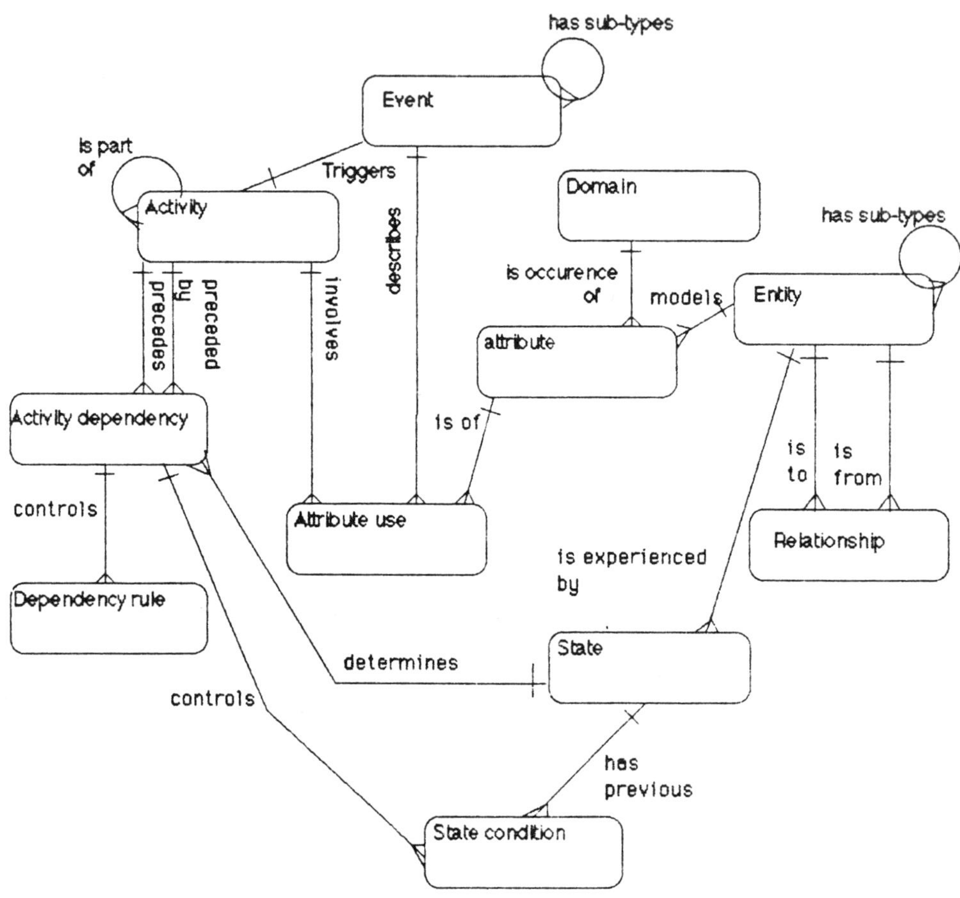

Figure 5.2 : Analysis data.

The design stage model of Figure 5.3 is heavily sub-hyphen typed. The entity function represents a structured grouping of logic from business functional area down to a single logic statement. The entity data group represents any grouping of data including screen, reports, files and views.

Figure 5.4 represents the programmer's view in the construction stage of the development cycle where the file sub-type of datagroup has been translated into a physical file definition while function and the screen and report sub-types of datagroup have been translated into programmes.

A major Scotish insurance company has followed Olle's work and produced conceptual models of each stage of the system development cycle. The project's brief was to develop a methodology which was technique independent. The conceptual data model approach taken, defines the contents of the deliverable products that are required from each stage of the development cycle. The methodology defines a sequence list of tasks which serves to populate the entire data model of the individual stages. The company is now free to choose the techniques appropriate to the task, the culture of the company and designed to populate a single object on a data model.

This approach to finding loosely coupled techniques which are integrated through the relationships of objects on the conceptual data models, gives the company freedom to change a technique as better ones are developed, without redesigning their methodology. The company can even employ prototyping as a technique for particular types of application whilst leaving the methodology task list and deliverables unchanged.

Translation of the objects of one stage into objects of the subsequent stage is incorporated within the rules of the translation technique supplemented by the skill of the translator. The lack of relationships between objects of different stages implies that there is no traceability between related object occurrences of the different stages. The relationships required for traceability between stages are coupled many to many relationships. Maintenance of these relationships falls to the lot of configuration management and version control. The relationships are not only across stage boundaries but because of the re-use of corporate data and common code the relationships cross system boundaries.

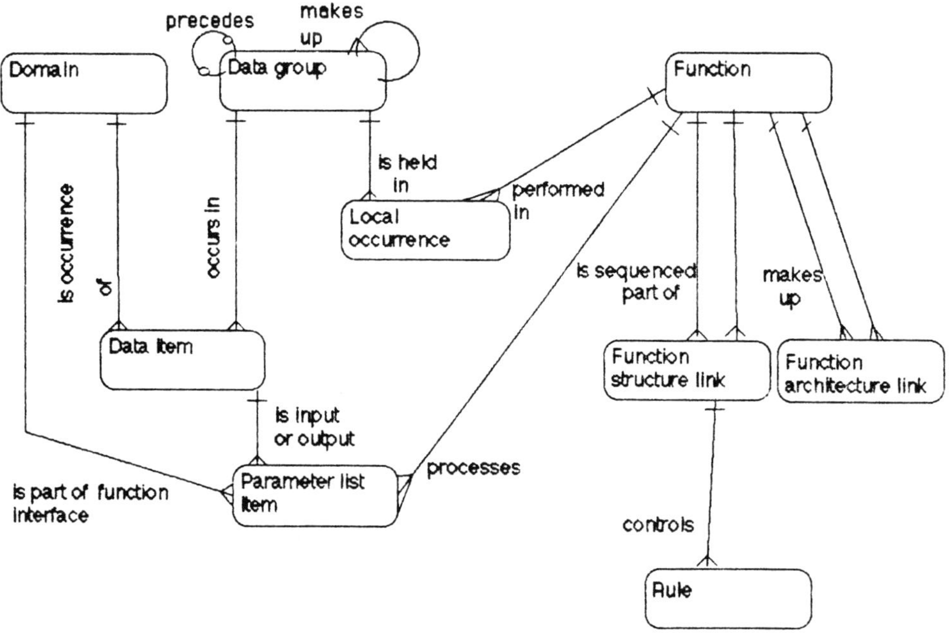

Figure 5.3 : Design data.

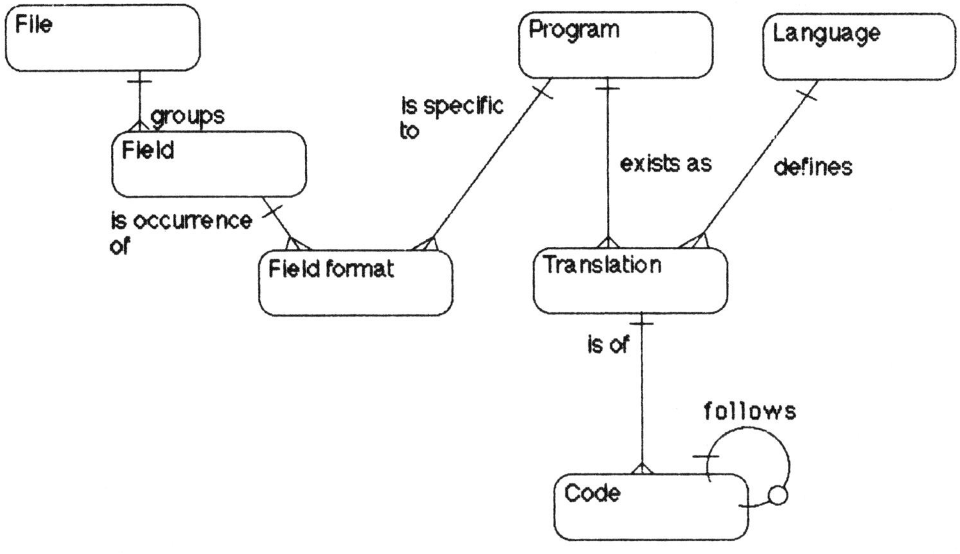

Figure 5.4 : Construction data.

In a recent report, David Kalinsky[3] describes in outline a CASE tool, CARD tools, Trace Builder, which is designed to check the consistency of trace relationships and to highlight those which potentially have been invalidated by a change in an object at some stage in the traceable chain.

Any successful IPSE tool is going to incorporate the rules of translation from one stage to another and maintain traceability.

4.2 Methodology convergence

A clear picture of the conceptual, development cycle and data models helps to understand the development of the methodologies. Yourdon, originally based on dataflow diagrams and program structure charts, has included the external behaviour of an event list and state transition diagrams. Data was represented by data flows and as unnormalised groupings in data stores. These views have been enhanced by a more rigorous entity relationship diagram.

Jackson's development method, JSD, identified unnormalised data objects upon which to build the behaviourial models of entity life cycles. These behaviourial models for anything other than the simple objects of a real time system, were too complex to instruct and Jackson has subsequently introduced full normalisation of the data group.

SSADM from its inception has incorporated the business behaviour, modelled by entity life histories, activities modelled in dataflow diagrams and information modelled in a logical data structure.

All these methods, and I anticipate information engineering will follow, are being developed to populate the whole of conceptual data models for the stages that they are designed to cover. SSADM is making a particular bid to become a *de facto* European, analysis methodology standard. It is particularly well placed to do so as it populates the majority of the conceptual analysis data model but one hopes that during its planned development, some of the techniques incorporated within it will be replaced by other more cohesive and complete ones. This move towards SSADM as a standard can be seen in recent press articles where both BIS and JMA have indicated an intention to incorporate or interface to SSADM.

4.3 Outstanding problems

The problem of defining rules for translation of objects in one stage to those in another has already been stated. The particular problem area is the translation of the analysis objects to design objects. Design itself is a finely balanced compromise of system usability, performance and adaptability. Each of these quality attributes is dependent upon physical parameters of the computer and communication systems as well as the logic and structure of the software elements. There are so many parameters to be considered that design is always a set of iterations.

CCTA commissioned some time ago, a study into the use of expert systems to perform database design optimisation, just a small part of the design process. The results of this study have not been published. One can only assume that the results gave no confidence that a design expert system could be developed at reasonable cost.

From a DP manager's point of view, the more pressing problem is how to accrue the benefits arising from the use of the methodology without losing the investment in existing application software.

4.4 Reverse engineering

Methodologies based on the Yourdon or Gane & Sarson have always advocated analysis of the current system. Reverse engineering starts in exactly the same way except the current system is entirely computer based. This therefore requires, not interview skills but analytical tools capable of presenting the current structure of the software in a way which is open to redesign and reconstruction. Several CASE tools have the capability of analysing existing source DDL to build a model of the installed physical database. Others such as PSL/PSA analyse existing source code to construct models of the programme structures. These t types of CASE tool populate parts of the design stage conceptual data mod

Re-engineering now requires the analyst to merge in the requi
the new system and then the designer to specify the restructuri
software components to maximise the re-use of existing software
new functionality. Automation of this process is still in

successful merging of reverse engineering tools in an I-CASE tool set will open an immense development, automation market.

4.5 CASE tool directions

Preceding sections have touched on changes which are taking place in current methodologies. Recognition of technique independent, conceptual data models has led Systematica to develop Virtual Software Factory with a fully configurable, rules base. This allows the methodology supported by VSF to change the techniques whilst leaving the deliverables' database unchanged. More analysts "and designers" workbenches will come to the market, offering this level of configurability. The integration of SDC stages, pioneered by IEF and taken up in different form by I-CASE tool sets will absorb a major portion of CASE tool research and development effort.

Vendors of upper CASE tools have sold their products into a financially wealthy market of large companies. Reverse engineering tools will open a market of mature middle size companies, where capitalising on current software investment is essential within constrained budgets. Re-engineering, if properly supported by CASE tools, will exert great influence on the development of methodologies. This can be seen in that reverse engineering is currently scheduled for incorporation within SSADM version 4+.

This chapter has not mentioned CASE tool support for expert system methodologies. Widespread use of expert systems is slow to come. The ever-growing number of expert system shells, targeted at particular, commercial sectors, should expand the market but they will fit with application generators in Lower CASE rather than support a generic expert system methodology. This may change if SSADM version 5, scheduled for release in 1991/92, incorporates expert systems successfully but the majority of DP development managers have interest in other areas besides expert systems.

5   SUMMARY

Methodologies are evolving systems which need to be enhanced to meet changing requirements and to be restructured on sound software engineering principles. This requires an open architecture of a technique independent, conceptual data model for each stage with rules for rigorous translation of objects between stages. This decoupling of stage models from techniques models should allow different techniques of reverse engineering, prototyping, object-oriented programming expert system design and others to be slotted into place in the methodology without causing fundamental re-design.

CASE tools will develop alongside the evolving methodologies. Technique independent, conceptual data model designs for upper CASE tools is fundamental to the production of integrated tools in an I-CASE set. This permits tools to be configurable to any selected methodology, technique set and to evolve at the same pace as methodologies.

6   REFERENCES

1   T Gilb (1988). Principles of Software Engineering Management. Addison Wesley

2   T W Olle (1988). Information Systems Methodologies. Addison Wesley

3   D Kalinsky, R Shilo, A Arnur (April 1989). Sunk without a   Trace. Systems International

Part Two

The User Perspective

6

CONFORMANCE APPRAISAL
OF CASE TOOLS

Manjeet S. Khaira
SSADM Research Centre,
Dept. of Computing, Birmingham Polytechnic

1   INTRODUCTION

The current growth in the supply of Computer-Aided Software Engineeing (CASE) tools to support the use of structured methods of analysis and design has many positive aspects. Not least it has led to interest in techniques for appraising products for "conformance to standards". That is, potential users of such tools, finding it an almost impossible task to fully evaluate every tool in a growing marketplace, are desperate to find some way of short-circuiting this process. In particular, they need to know what a statement such as "provides comprehensive support for SSADM techniques" actually means (i.e. what is comprehensive, what is support and what techniques). Only by finding answers to these questions can the users make confident decisions about investment in CASE.

The aim of this paper is to discuss the rationale behind conformance appraisal by using the SSADM Support Tools Conformance Appraisal Scheme as an example. This scheme, established within the SSADM Research Centre (SRC) at Birmingham Polytechnic, aims to appraise the level of support given to SSADM by current and future offerings in the CASE tools area. The appraisal is to be done by utilising a formal model of SSADM as a basis for a series of conformance tests. These tests will be carried out by staff at the SRC, and results, in terms of achieved "star ratings" will be made available to both the tool supplier and to the Central Computers and Telecommunications Agency (CCTA) who manage SSADM. CCTA will make the conformance rating public via their normal channels.

A further aim of the scheme is to improve the quality of support tools on the market by making public the criteria for achieving higher levels of star ratings. It is anticipated that pressure from users for tools to meet these criteria will stimulate a buoyant market even further.

2   BACKGROUND TO CONFORMANCE APPRAISAL FOR SSADM

In order to provide justification for the scheme one needs to look at the current situation regarding SSADM. The use of SSADM is widespread because it provides the benefits of improved quality and productivity in systems development and maintenance. This widespread use has prompted the development and commercial availability of many CASE tools which are increasingly becoming powerful and sophisticated. The SSADM CASE tools market is now differentiated in that different tools exist to support the needs of both casual users and dedicated practitioners.

From the user perspective, investment in CASE tools is costly and requires careful planning. Users are looking for products which will protect their investment through the support of standards and provide the flexibility of incremental growth. However, they do not have the resources or the time to carry out in-depth product evaluations for themselves.

On the other hand, a certain amount of uncertainty exists as far as suppliers are concerned. There is as yet no definitive set of requirements for CASE tools to support SSADM. The nearest thing is the official SSADM Reference Manual, published by the National Computing Centre. This, however, is not in the right form for a requirements specification and a lot of further effort is required to use it to formulate a model for CASE tools. Further, suppliers need to be able to differentiate their products from others on the market.

It is due to this background that a conformance appraisal scheme is required to assist buyers and suppliers of CASE tools. It is necessary to make it easier for users to buy, by helping to clarify the selection process, and for suppliers to sell, by introducing a rating system supported by a published specification. By carrying out conformance checks the scheme will describes to users the SSADM support features they will find in conforming products, and assist tool developers to provide them.

The CCTA and the SRC see the scheme as one of crucial importance for the SSADM CASE tool market. It will enable the controlled maturation of an already volatile and proliferated market. The importance of the scheme is expected to increase as UK standards are subsumed into developing European based approaches.

Based on this background, the Conformance Appraisal for SSADM Support Tools has the following objectives:

- to facilitate the buying and selling of support tools;

- to provide a mechanism for conformance testing support tools;

- to establish a minimum set of requirements for SSADM support tools at a number of levels of conformance;

- to provide commercial and educational organisations with a model for development and research;

- to define achievable criteria for the appraisal of currently available commercial SSADM CASE tools;

- to offer an impartial and independent appraisal service, with provision for pre-evaluation of products.

3   THE BASIS FOR CONFORMANCE APPRAISAL

SSADM has great potential for computer support. Consider the three views of a system provided in SSADM - the functions (dataflow diagramming), the data (logical data structuring), and entity life histories. These constitute a tightly coupled set of concepts which are ideally suited to computer support. The information content and the semantics of these concepts are well understood and thus the three views and their interdependencies can be represented as a model appropriate for a design database schema. These concepts are illustrated in Figures 6.1 and 6.2. This type of model not only defines much of the syntax and semantics of SSADM, but also graphically represents the types of completeness and consistency checks which are required. The same model can be used to express the requirements for support tools for SSADM.

A detailed Entity-Relationship-Attribute (ERA) model has been constructed by CCTA for version 3 of SSADM. CCTA and the SRC have developed a model that constitutes a level of abstraction from this ERA model and forms the basis for the conformance appraisal mechanisms. This conformance appraisal model is the most appropriate way of expressing the concepts of the current version of SSADM, whose structural, technical and documentation standards are otherwise represented in the current NCC SSADM V3.0 Reference Manual published by the National Computing Centre (NCC). The model also provides a way of illustrating the interdependencies between the concepts and the information content of these concepts and interdependencies. The value of this approach is that it affords a good way of understanding the nature of SSADM, and provides a good model for comparison with computer support tool data dictionary components.

The model on its own is not sufficient to carry out the appraisal process. It needs to be supported by detailed guidelines to clarify the meaning and inter-relationships of the various concepts it embodies. Also, the model tends to be a static view of the information content without much regard to the processing requirements of a CASE tool. For example, the model does not state anything about the sort of reporting, validation, consistency and completeness checking facilities to be included in a tool. Thus, apart from criteria for the syntax and semantics of the various concepts and their inter-relationships that can be derived from the model, a further set of criteria have been developed to define the processing requirements of CASE tools. Also, to facilitate the assessment task, a detailed questionnaire based on the two sets of criteria requiring "yes/no" answers has been developed. This questionnaire will enable the CASE tool suppliers to gauge the exact degree of conformance of their product before formal submission for certification. The next section illustrates how the questionnaire was developed for criteria based on the conformance model.

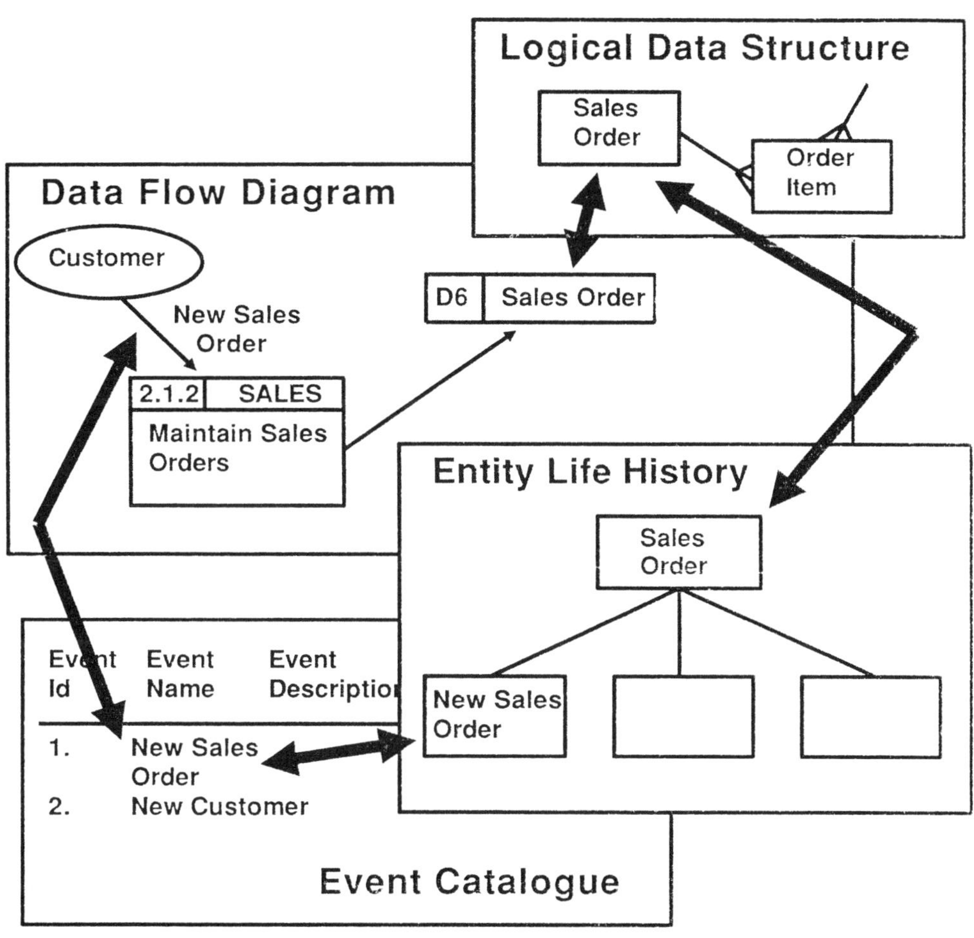

Figure 6.1 : The integration of SSADM techniques.

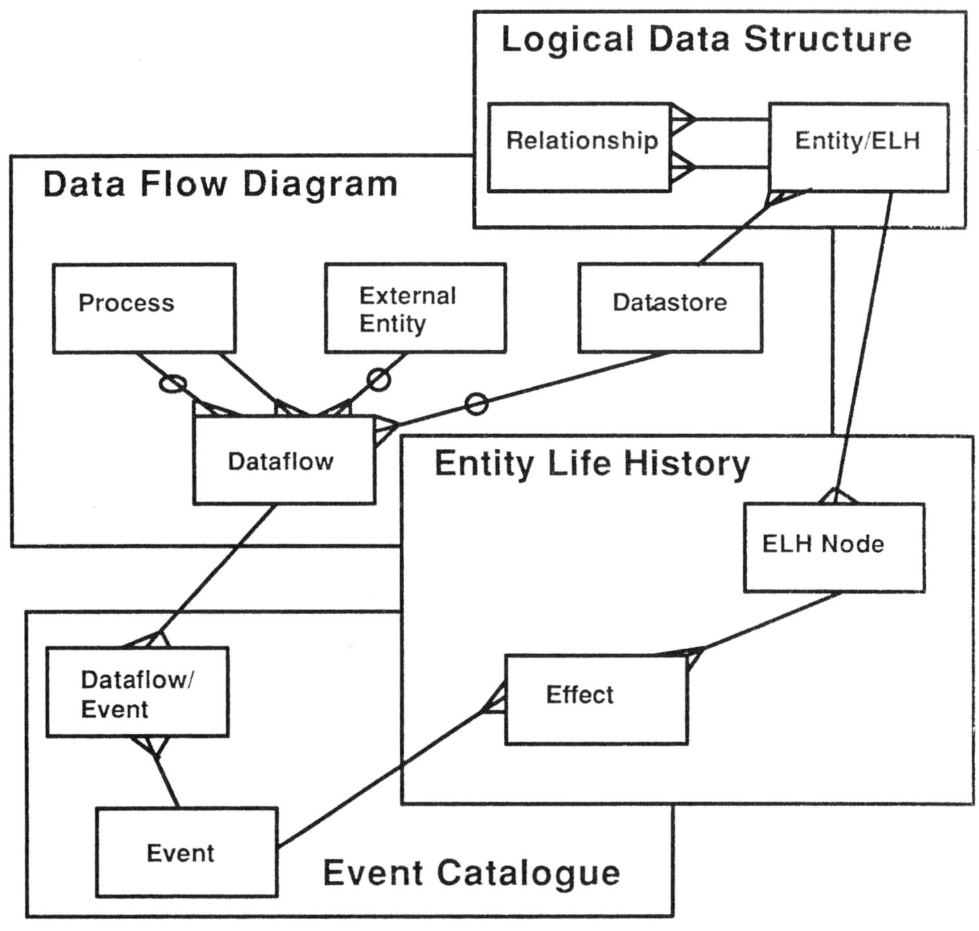

Figure 6.2 : A schematic view of interrelationships between SSADM concepts.

3.1 Questionnaire development

The notation used in the conformance model will first be briefly introduced. Basically, the model is an Entity-Relationship Diagram where each box with rounded corners represents a distinct entity (a significant type of thing about which information needs to be held). In Figure 6.3 there are two such entities labelled DATAFLOW DIAGRAM and SYSTEM. Such names are important because they form a useful vocabulary of standard terms within SSADM and serve as labels for those things which are defined in the model. The size of each box is chosen for convenience and has no significance in itself.

There is an important relationship between a SYSTEM and a DATAFLOW DIAGRAM and is shown by the line connecting them. Such relationship lines can be read from either end as sentences. The two sentences which decribe this pair of complementary relationships are read from the diagram as follows:

- The sentence begins with "Each" because the line on the diagram is making a statement that applies to every individual instance of DATAFLOW DIAGRAM that may occur in a system.

- "DATAFLOW DIAGRAM" is in block capitals to signify that these words refer to some type of thing defined within the model. This helps to reserve the use of block capitals for such labels in order to distinguish them from similar words which may be used without such implications.

- The words "must be" imply that no instance of DATAFLOW DIAGRAM may exist without a relationship of this type. i.e. without being "for" some specific SYSTEM. Thus the relationship is seen to be mandatory for the entity DATAFLOW DIAGRAM. Such mandatory relationships are shown on the diagram with a line which is solid at the end nearest the subject entity, i.e. the one that this sentence is helping to describe. A broken line here would mean that the relationship is optional and the words "may be" would be used instead.

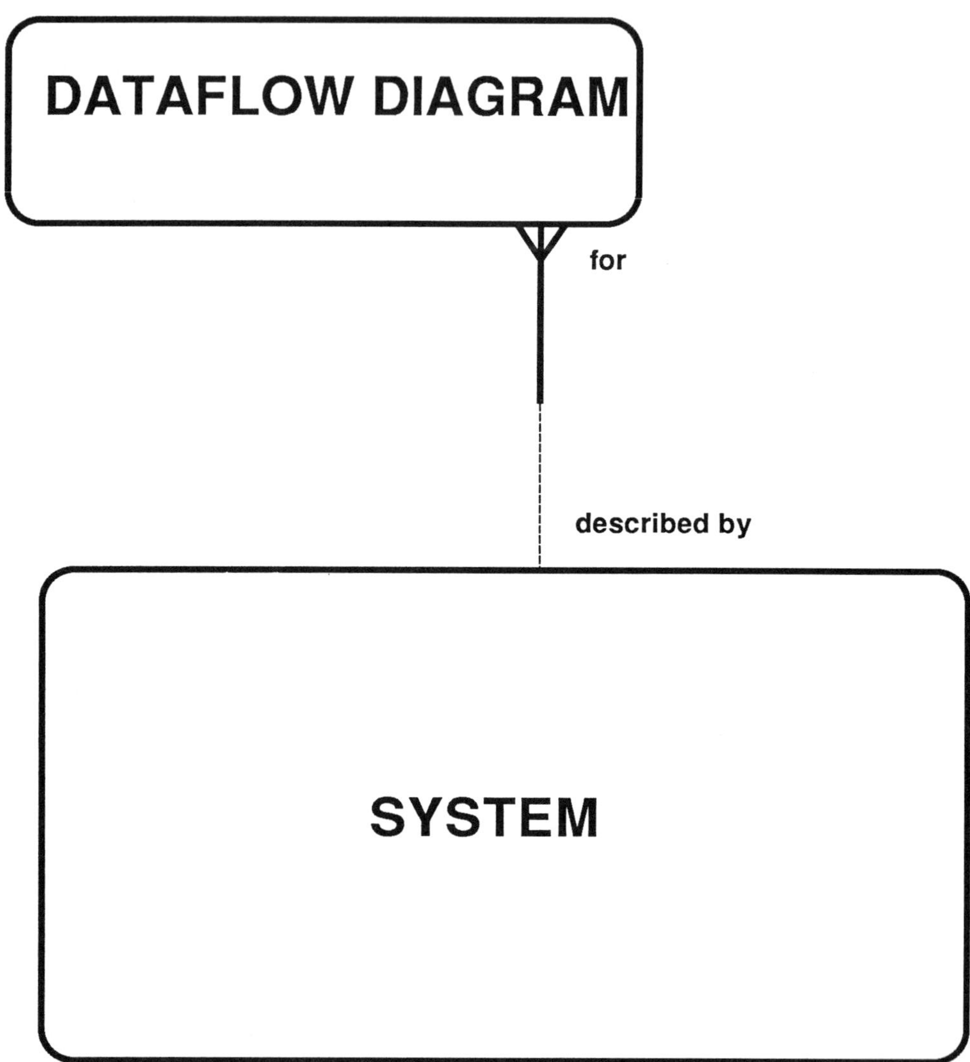

Figure 6.3 : Notation used in Entity-Relationship Diagram.

- The next word "for", is a link phrase chosen to add meaning to the relationship, and to turn it into a sentence that makes sense. In this case the meaning is obvious, but in some cases, as many as five or six words may be needed to convey the right understanding to the reader.

- The words "one and only one" are most important, in that they give a categoric assurance that there is one and only one SYSTEM related in this way to any given DATAFLOW DIAGRAM. This means that there is just one set of details such as identity, description etc. held for each SYSTEM which applies to any given instance of DATAFLOW DIAGRAM.

- Finally we have the name of the object entity, i.e. the one in the box at the far end of the line, which in this case is "SYSTEM".

If the diagram is looked at from the viewpoint of the SYSTEM we find a rather different relationship. First we see that the line is broken at this end, so we have:

"Each SYSTEM may be described by ...."

Now we look to the point at which the line joins on to the object entity, which from this viewpoint is "DATAFLOW DIAGRAM". Here we find a "crows foot symbol" as it is called. This implies that "one or more" instances of that entity may be involved. Hence the full sentence is:

"Each SYSTEM may be described by one or more DATAFLOW DIAGRAMS."

Additional notation is provided to enrich the model, but detailed discussion of that is outside the scope of this paper. Taking the above sentences, it is very easy to convert them into questions for the CASE tool supplier to answer. For example the first sentence can be turned into a question as follows:

"Does your SSADM Support Tool ensure that each DATAFLOW DIAGRAM belongs to one and only one SYSTEM (yes/no) ?"

In this way every single relationship on the model is converted to two question. Further questions relate to the minimum set of attributes needed to define various entities on the model and the object representations of the entities if they appear as parts of diagrams or as parts of the SSADM form set.

The questions were then grouped according to the various levels of conformance described later.

3.2 The Scope of the criteria

The criteria do not intrinsically cover aspects of usability, performance or reliability, and these features will provide supppliers with opportunities for product differentiation. These aspects are already well covered in independent appraisal criteria. The certification criteria will enable suppliers, users and the SRC to assess the following CASE tool product features:

- the structure and content of SSADM supported by the product;

- the product's adherence to SSADM documentation standards in diagramming tools, textual input forms, plotted diagrams and printed reports and, most importantly,

- the existence of, or potential for, a full range of completeness and consistency checks to produce lists, standard SSADM catalogues and more complex, comparative reports. These should detail what is inconsistent or missing, rather than merely list what is present.

4   LEVELS OF CONFORMANCE

Clearly, current tools do not all provide equal capability, and it is not the CCTA's intention to create a situation where product developers would be unable to meet both the requirement for SSADM support and achieve the degree of product differentiation necessary to claim sufficient market share. CCTA seeks a differentiated market and actively encourages suppliers to move towards wider and deeper levels of support in an expanding market place.

In order too propagate these aims, the scheme provides four levels of conformance, and these can be appropriately expressed as a set of "star ratings". The differentiation between the levels, and the rationale for each is described in more detail later in this section. The star ratings are an assessment of both mandatory and desirable features within clearly defined levels of support. This has two major advantages:

- the users will have a clear understanding of which facilities will be present at each level of rating, and

- vendors will know which changes to their product will improve their product's rating.

To facilitate this, the broad structure of the rating system is this. Each level of conformance will consist of a number of mandatory features - which must be present to achieve the rating. In addition, there will be a number of desirable features which ideally should be present. To achieve the next higher level of approval, all mandatory and desirable features from the level below must be present, together with any mandatory features specific to the higher level.

However, to reflect the value of desirable features in those tools which may not be capable of satisfying all the requirements of a higher star rating, a system of supplementary indicators will be employed to indicate which desirable features are supported, and in which category they fall. This will provide an incentive for vendors to extend their product's capabilities, and hence its value to practitioners, even in those cases where the underlying architecture - or financial constraints - would make it unlikely that a full higher star rating could be achieved.

A detailed definition of the requirement, and the way in which products will be assessed against it will be available as part of the SRC appraisal service. For the purpose of this paper, the "star ratings" can be summarised thus:

- The product must have the fundamental capabilities of a sophisticated drawing tool plus primitive file structure.

- An intra-techniques checking facility is required, e.g. a datastore to datastore flow is identified as not permissible. However, no cross knowledge need exist between, for example, a datastore and its related LDS structure.

- Such a product requires:

  1. an ability to provide "cross technique" validation;

  2. support for those SSADM processes which involve modifying syntactically correct diagrams (e.g. logicalization, validation), and;

  3. the ability to hold in a support tool's data dictionary the data content of SSADM "forms".

- Directs SSADM stages and steps by "knowing" which inputs are needed before a step can commence. It also must be able to reproduce SSADM forms for completion on screen, and to automate the major part of this form filling.

5   PUBLICATION OF RESULTS

When the results of a conformance appraisal test have been made available to CCTA by the SRC, it will issue an appropriate conformance certificate to the supplier showing the "star rating" achieved by the submitted product - subject to its achieving the minimum 1* level of support.

CCTA will also make public, by an appropriate mechanism, the "star ratings" achieved by submitted tools. This will fulfil the requirement to let potential buyers know to what extent submitted products support SSADM.

When they have received their conformance certificate, suppliers may use the certificate, and the associated star rating, in any way they see fit.

6   CONCLUSION

The importance of such a scheme cannot be overemphasised. The whole philosophy behind it is to do with the importance of following standards. Which is made even more important if we consider "the Distributed Development Environment". If a certain standard is selected for systems development then the CASE tool should support it rigorously. Non-conformance at best causes inconsistencies in development practice and at worst invalidates the whole reason for using a particular method(ology) in the first place.

The SSADM Support Tool Conformance Scheme illustrates that objective assessment can be carried out without undermining CASE tool supplier freedom and at the same time push the market to deliver products to meet buyer requirements and reduce the level of uncertainty. The scheme also illustrates that the approach can be applied to other methods where there is a proliferation of CASE tools. However, the caveats are that such a scheme must ensure objectivity and must be administered by an independent body. The requirements therefore are a model for conformance that embodies the concepts embedded in a method and the casting aside of any hangups about the functionality and usability issues.

7   ACKNOWLEDGEMENTS

This chapter contains extracts from the "SSADM Support Tools Conformance Appraisal Scheme" publication produced by CCTA and the SRC. Also the author would like to acknowledge the assistance provided by Tony Jenkins, head of the SRC, towards the production of this chapter.

7

COMPUTER AIDED SUPPORT IN DESIGNING AND BUILDING A DISTRIBUTED SYSTEM USING INGRES

John Burke
Principal Consultant SD-Scicon

1 INTRODUCTION

SD-Scicon is an international systems house involved in the implementation of large, turnkey systems for government, defence, industrial and commercially based clients.

Whilst the company is often involved in the very early stages of specification, where the initial business plan, operational requirements and data and function analysis (SSADM stages 1, 2 and 3) are produced, it is often the case that these analysis have been performed and the project is now being offered to competitive tender for full implementation or an initial technical design study leading to implementation.

An increasing factor in this environment is that these implementations rely more on the use of third party software - relational databases such as INGRES and the productivity tools such as screen and forms generators and 4GLs that go with them. Whilst not fundamentally altering the design process it flavours it both advantageously and disadvantageously.

A further factor now is that increasingly the systems implemented are no longer installed on a single machine but consist of networks of machines using either the distributed aspects of the database product or application software to maintain replica or slave copies of the database.

The focus in this paper is therefore on the types of computer aided support required in this environment of analysing the initial position and proceeding further through logical data and process design to the physical design and implementation of the system (SSADM stages 4,5 and 6 onwards). It is in many cases intended as a list of desirable facilities that should be considered by those who develop CASE tools where the current emphasis seems to be on totally fulfilling the requirements of less complicated requirements rather than partially fulfilling those of a more complex nature.

2   ANALYSIS OF THE REQUIREMENT

2.1 Main analysis requirements

Analysis of the requirement depends to a great deal on the level of detail already collected and how the information is structured.

Traditionally, operational requirements consisted of a series of statements defining the functions to be performed by the system in sometimes varying detail, together with figures describing the expected system loadings.

Now these English documents are often accompanied by a set of generic SSADM type documentation :

- Entity life histories

- Dataflow diagrams

- Output from a data dictionary

- Function catalogues

The inclusion of this information should provide a greater degree of assurance that the requirement has been properly addressed and that there are fewer inconsistencies. However, due to the greater amount of information collected it is often the case that more inconsistencies are introduced between the formal documentation and the English text due to not keeping the information current. As systems increase in complexity CASE support for this initial analysis is becoming increasingly important in producing a consistent requirement. It is also important to tie the narrative to the diagrammatic information in such a way that inconsistencies can be resolved.

An important facility that should be added to a CASE tool that allows major wordprocessing activities should be a free text retrieval system that will allow the English text to be interrogated and cross references obtained to the formal tabled and diagrammatic information.

This obviously provides a problem when the tools used to produce a requirement are incompatible to those used to analyse that requirement. In this case optical scanning of all documents into a free-text database is a poorer alternative.

2.2 Additional analysis

When these requirements are for "information" systems where there is a great deal of screen based user interaction the information most needed to proceed to an initial system sizing is often missing. This is the MMI or Functional Specification which details the actual screens and user interactions with the system.

This often occurs for a number of reasons, the better ones being that the person procuring the system does not wish to prejudice the MMI towards features of particular hardware or software packages.

However, this does raise problems in that the implementation time and amount of resource needed to fulfil a particular function in a function catalogue may vary widely depending on the user interface.

For instance, if an action requires confirmation and the user insists that a second screen is presented to perform the confirmation rather than a prompt and function key confirmation, then the system utilisation profile will be very different.

In a slightly less obvious way, many 4GLs provide "table" view facilities, where replicated data may be scrolled within a window on the screen. For certain types of user this form of display is not appropriate and extra screens need to be paged through actively to display the data. This again affects the system utilisation profile and implementation time.

Similarly, if the amount of data displayed on each screen is not specified accurately, then with a relational database this will affect the number of rows retrieved from different tables leading to uncertanties in the amount of processing required.

Also inaccuracies in the number of screens leads to inaccuracies in the image sizes generated, memory requirements and the amount of paging.

3   FUNCTIONAL SPECIFICATION

3.1 General

With the functional specification it is important to link the hardcopy screens, specimen reports and forms which are produced for the specification as easily as possible to the eventual code. To this end 4GL screen editors and report generators are useful in that they produce a textual description of each field and the automatic validation undertaken as well as code templates. There should also be an overlap between any prototyping work and the final functional specification.

The functional specification should also be the embryo user manual.

So the production of a Functional Specification either as part of a proposal or as the next stage of a contract needs at least the following support :

3.2 Prototyping

The use of a relational database system such as INGRES and its associated tools ABF, VIFRED and OSL is useful in prototyping the user interface to the system.

VIFRED allows the rapid generation and editing of the screens to be used in the system and the reports produced are suitable for inclusion in the functional specification.

ABF and OSL allow the rapid linking together of these screens and the simulation of genuine user transactions with a test database.

In using these tools our primary objective is to specify the system in such a manner that the user interface is unambiguous and the user is able to see for himself the limitations and features of the standard interface. This is so because depending on the type of system being built, the amount of work that can be carried forward directly to the later stages of implementation is very variable. In most cases a 4GL, although much quicker to implement provides an inefficient final solution. Also when distributed or multi-nodal aspects are taken into consideration the implementor may need to drop down to a 3GL.

4 PHYSICAL DESIGN

4.1 General

Once the Functional Specification has been determined it is necessary to continue the physical design. Normally, for large systems, a three level approach is adopted. The top level attempts to complete the physical database design, and decompose the system into subsystems and individual processes with all inter-process messages defined. The next level defines the internals of each process and the third consists of the actual coding, testing and integration.

4.2 Level 1 Design

Database design and performance modelling support

With the use of a relational database it is much more important to obtain actual benchmark results than with older record oriented systems.

Previously it was fairly easy to count the number of disc accesses. Now queries are more complex and the work performed for each query is less easy to calculate. The implementor is rarely faced with a simple repetitive set of transactions since users are now often presented with *ad hoc* search facilities. Often the time taken by the query parser itself is significant and it is not always possible to predict the type of search that will be generated. It is important to produce, at an early stage, a prototype physical database populated with the correct distribution of data ranges to allow performance measurements to be run.

It is possible to produce the database definitions reasonably quickly manually by use of a data dictionary although at present all of the available data dictionaries investigated require more manual intervention than we would like. Also there is rarely a match between the dictionary used in the initial requirements analysis stage and that chosen for the final implementation. A common standard will obviously alleviate this problem as will the ability to generate database schemas from entity-relationship diagrams.

Another major weakness in the area is in populating of test databases once they have been generated. Although it is possible to write simple scripts within the terminal monitor to populate tables with the correct statistical distribution of, for instance, names, it is a long process for a complex database. There is room for a tool that would, from a dictionary of names, addresses, common English words and the like create a realistic test database from the statistical information provided. This is also applicable to the prototyping field.

Once the test database has been populated, generation of test queries is straightforward by use of the terminal monitor and SQL scripts. The INGRES terminal monitor is reasonably good in allowing query plans to be examined and calibration results themselves to be fed into results tables for further analysis.

Physical Process Design

The idea is to redefine the intial logical functions contained in the function catalogue into more comfortably defined 'machine' functions so that each subsystem eventually holds a non-overlapping set of functions.

During this process the cross-referencing of new to old functions, the generation of interfaces between the subsystems (messages) and the description of the new functions should all be aided by database support. This database of functions and their decompositions should form part of any comprehensive CASE environment.

This process of decomposition should then be applied to each subsystem. Each subsystem is subdivided into processes (individual programs or modules or libraries) which will normally communicate via interprocess messages (e.g. VMS mailbox messages).

In summary during this process one would expect that a well designed CASE tool would allow the design team to perform the following exercises :

- Take the SSADM (or similar) output consisting of Entity Life Histories (ELH), function catalogues and CLDDs and build the physical database schema from the attribute and entity models with normalisation and relaxation facilities and populate test databases with the correct statistical mix of data.

- Decide initially on the subsystems that are going to be used and the nodes on which they will reside.

- For each function in the function catalogue list which physical entities are created /deleted/updated.

- Allocate each function to a single subsystem or define a function in terms of several others if it spans more than one subsystem. If a function is split define the interprocess messages that must link it ideally in a form that will allow code to be generated from the message templates.

- Produce summaries of :

  - functions performed by each subsystem

  - interprocess messages between subsystems

  - database tables updated by each subsystem

  - cross-references to each initial function

  - allow me to define naming conventions for programs,messages, files and databases.

The above facilities should be available at both the high and lower design levels and it should be possible to regress to the higher level, make alterations and then be presented with a set of changes that need to be made at a lower level. It is important that these changes are not made automatically but must at least be acknowledged by the designer(s) before the complete change is committed. It should also be possible easily to "roll-back" any undesirable changes.

At this point, for each program there should be a specification consisting of:

- a list of functions serviced with reference to the messages and database updates performed for each function.

- reference lists of messages in and out and files and database tables read or updated.

Completeness and Consistency Checking

The consistency checking that should now be possible from this information is the following:

- Logical path testing of inter-process messages.

  This will vary in sophistication depending on the level of detail entered at the previous stage. At least it should ensure that each message received by a process elicits a reply which itself may be acknowledged. If sequencing information is added then a tree of the possible message exchanges may be generated since it is not practical at this stage to attempt to simulate conditional tests when a choice of messages is generated.

- Timeout conditions, simulating communications failures.

  This can be tested to the same level of sophistication as normal message exchanges.

- Coverage of all logical functions.

- Cross references of database data. If all functions are covered and some data is not referenced then exception reports may be generated questioning the relevance of the data.

Performance Prediction

At this point it should also be possible to start to get a better feel for volumetrics. There should be scope within the function list within a program to estimate the number of iterations per hour,the processing time and amount of I/O activity per iteration. In estimating the I/O activity there is scope in linking the query optimiser and the test database to obtain accurate estimates.

Once this information is collected there is scope for further manipulation. For instance, it should be possible to alter the system configuration such as the number of discs, placement of tables on discs and processor power and examine the results either in terms of overall utilisation or individually observed function times.

Integration Plans

From the level 1 design information it should also be possible to generate, at least in part, integration plans.

For complex systems it is often desirable to deliver the system in a number of phases. It should be possible to postulate a number of subsets of the system for delivery, either by a list of functions or some other criterion and have presented an integration plan showing which programs need to be developed first and what deadlocks or dummy processes will have to be used.

4.3 Level 2 design

This stage of development is the definition of each discrete program to a detailed level by various means

e.g. Jackson diagrams pseudocode

Depending on the method chosen, the support needed will be different. For a more complex system with a bias to multithreading or asynchronous events a pseudocode decomposition is often the most effective. Again it should be possible to take the output directly from the level above and detail each function to a lower level.

At this point it is important to have a complete database, interprocess message and screen realisations to allow correct references to be made in the pseudocode.

The design document should be logically one document and in viewing it the viewer should just specify the level to which he wishes to descend.

It should be possible to produce a Level 2 report document which :

- defines all functions in terms of pseudo-code

- lists all interprocess messages

- lists all database accesses - to table level

- lists all procedure definitions and calls

4.4 Level 3 design

At this stage code is being generated and tested for the first time requiring different support tools.

Code Generators

Up to this point, possibly due to the nature of the systems being developed by the area of the company, it has been found that general purpose code generators are neither applicable nor available although specially developed ones have been of use for producing certain repetitive data driven code and for updating multiple copies of databases where the use of INGRES/STAR, the distributed element of INGRES has not been appropriate.

To aid code generation the minimum support environment should be the provision of program skeletons to standardise startup, closedown, error handling and operating system specific functions.

With this approach and the advent of stored procedures, it is the intention that that these process skeletons will provide a harness for code that will map directly to the pseudocode which will service each message and make code generation more feasible in complex systems.

Code management

This is obviously a necessity. Current projects use a number of products such as CMS and MMS on Digital equipment. The advent of stored procedures within relational databases and relaxation of maximum row sizes within databases such as INGRES will soon start to alter this code management function especially in more complex systems. It will be possible to maintain dictionaries, screen formats, database schemas and code modules as entities within a single database .

This will become more important as distributed databases become more common, since a perennial problem with multi-node systems is how to update software on all nodes whilst maintaining system integrity. Stored procedures, coupled with a two-phase commit mechanism will alleviate this problem.

5   SUMMARY

In summary, it seems that the most promising approach for the production of CASE tools for large complicated systems which use a relational database as part of the final system (or even not) is for the database supplier to produce a powerful dictionary which may be used as the core of the system within which he defines such objects as forms, reports, physical database generation schema and perhaps stored procedures and support for recognised methodologies.

In addition an open interface to this dictionary allows separate suppliers and developers to define their own object types and generate their own specialised tools which by the nature of the different application areas will have different bias, such as those outlined above which would include :

- Data capture into a free-text database facilities,

- Test database generation and population with realistic data,

- Logical to Physical function decomposition and cross-referencing to the "real" user interface,

- Subsystem decomposition and interprocess definition,

- Early "continuity" testing of interprocess messages and timeout and communications failure scenarios,

- Integration plans based on lists of functions and some level of code generation.

8

CASE TOOL USAGE FOR SYSTEMS ANALYSIS/DESIGN

DFA Piesse
Azimuth Software Ltd

1   STRENGTHS AND WEAKNESSES

As an analyst workbench EXCELERATOR supports top-down and bottom-up analysis and design. An add-on product allows the ability to perform physical database design, most recently with DB2, with links to the DB2 catalogue.

Facilities are provided to aid functional decomposition, data modelling and dataflow analysis for logical and physical design.

The software provides facilities by use of and underlying CAD process to produce graphics for dataflow deagrams, data models and structure diagrams. The graphics feature is very powerful but suffers in functionality if shapes are customized as it loses the level balancing capability. A common customization is to change the shapes to support LBMS (Learmonth and Burchett Methodology). The new release is addressing the weakness of shape customisation and is a root change to the CAD infrastructure.

In addition to the graphics definitions and descriptions of data are held in a textual format, both graphics and text being linked to an internal dictionary. Features provide ability to do level balancing and normalisation checks to verify data structures are in third normal form. This is actually achieved by flagging the table as normalized and a matrix is returned with anomalies. Import and export facilities provide a good file-gateway to communicate with outside systems.

EXCELERATOR in the long term will help organizations to head towards consistency. Multiple versions of design can be stored and archived.

A major strength of EXCELERATOR is the ability to change the original product simply and inexpensively using the customization and programming interface tools provided. Thus user needs can be addressed without a great deal of encumbrance. For organizations such as large banks who reside in multi-vendor environments this is a major benefit. Much of the customization takes place on the dictionary.

A second major strength of EXCELERATOR is the open architecture concept where it can support most methodologies and conventions, several databases and their respective dictionaries, code generators such as TELON, APS, project management tools such as PMW and test facilities such as Micro-Focus COBOL Workbench. The ability to accommodate these on a workstation basis is in keeping with the IBM WASE (Workstation Assisted Systems Engineering) standard. This supports front-end workstations tightly coupled to mainframe-based back-end code and database generations.

A third strength of the analyst workbench is the superb tutorial.

Weaknesses of the analyst workbench are external to the graphics functions. Printing is very hard to use and often results in the editing of print-files. Screen design has no prototyping facilities and menus cannot be created. Very primitive chaining allows the linking of screens together. Internal security could be improved with only one level of password. On the extended analysis the reports are not always readable. On the graphics the ability to move the labels around is a much desired feature. Release 1.9 (GRANITE) will provide much more functionality. The author had intended to beta test the new release before this paper but the release was delayed.

Users can expect a 10% productivity gain for diagrams/charts, balancing flows, normalization, enforcement of standards such as METHOD/1 and reduced corporate dictionary keying. This is providing you are not in an application package environment where the logical design has not been done. This important anomaly applies to all CASE tools and is addressed later in the paper.

Better communication is achieved at the project level on a peer to peer basis which makes impact of change information more readily accessible to the users. The dictionary allows information building at the project and corporate level.

Purchasing of large packages, especially COBOL, greatly change the EXCELERATOR environment. Links to Micro-Focus COBOL assist here.

Designers in a package environment will generally pick up the code and run on a physical basis leaving data management and dictionary personnel to re-key, re-engineer and reverse engineer the system into a logical design. This can be a large re-key effort.

This paper will discuss the use of EXCELERATOR in a large organization and address the following key issues:

a) ADDRESSING THE ENVIRONMENT
b) DATA DICTIONARY MANAGEMENT
c) STANDARDS ENFORCEMENT
d) DATABASE MANAGEMENT
e) EXPERT SYSTEM INTERFACE
f) SECURITY INTERFACES
g) FUTURE ADDITIONS

2 ENVIRONMENT

Selection of EXCELERATOR as a CASE tool for large organizations is tantamount to creating home-spun I-CASE for short-term planning, a cottage industry within the Data Management Group.

Implementation of intergrated CASE methodologies in large organizations with multiple technologies is not recommended by the author due to the amount of customization required to support the environment. I-CASE concepts are best retained for a future platform as CASE technology matures.

Smaller organizations with a confirmed set direction e.g. a company with SYBASE, VAX and 4GL development tools may utilize an integrated CASE system such as CREON which provides the complete methodology. This methodology supports the full life cycle of a system from planning, analysis and design to code generation and maintenance. This also includes documentation generators, project management aids and database generators.

In either CASE situation this paper places a very strong emphasis on dictionary concepts.

A typical environment in a large organization is illustrated below.

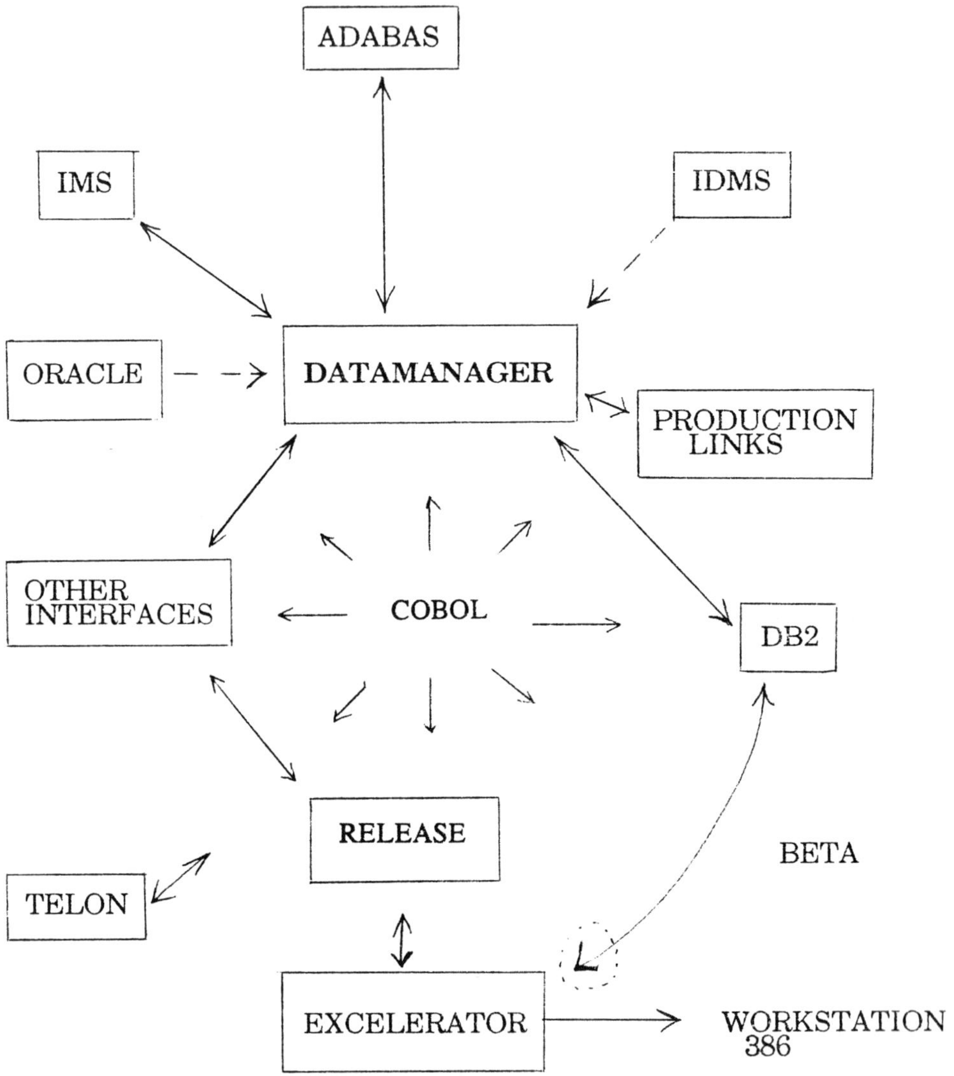

Figure 8.1 : Multi - product linkages.

3   DICTIONARIES

Every organization should have a corporate dictionary to control the data resource and some cases to generate building blocks for applications. EXCELERATOR provides a local dictionary interface on a project basis to the corporate dictionary.

It is important to have a strategic link between the local and corporate dictionaries and not to allow updating across project peer levels. All updates should be forced to the corporate dictionary via the local dictionary using appropriate locking mechanisms. Just using import/export facilities to move data is not sufficient. Assuming a traditional corporate dictionary such as DATAMANAGER, and not object-oriented as alluded to later, use of the CUSTOMER software provide strength to provide a strategic link. An EXCELERATOR user should always customize the links by this route and avoid writing their own customization routines or using public domain software links. This is because when the vendor changes the EXCELERATOR dictionary format all strategic links using CUSTOMISER will have a smooth upgrade whereas a home built routine will be subject to disruption. Public domain software is also a problem because of the lack of upgrade, support and openess to virus infection.

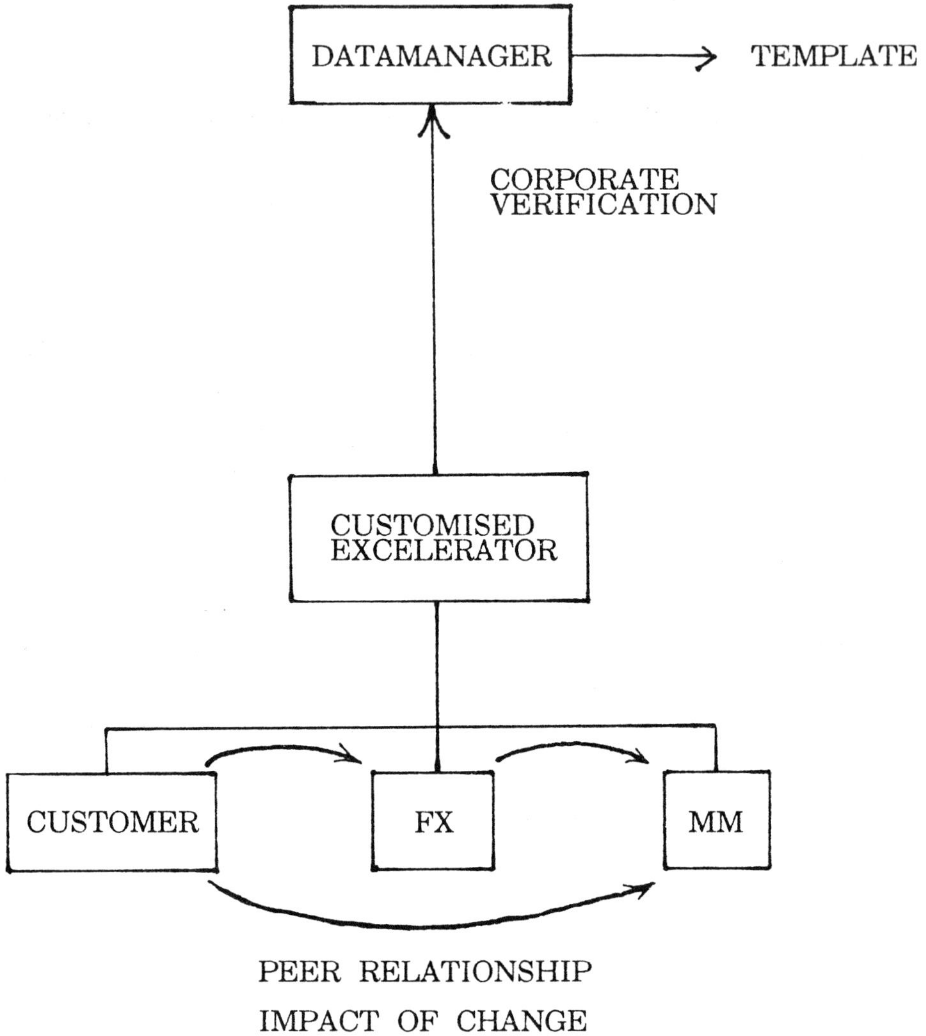

Figure 8.2 : Project environment.

The dictionary has a large role to play in distributed architectures. Co-ordinating the computerized knowledge base across a large development or information engineering effort is best done utilizing distributed architectures.

This is the ability to network EXCELERATOR. In larger projects the AS400 could be used to store the project dictionaries using the VDAM type features of EXCELERATOR where the PC accesses larger volumes of data stored on a host. This would enable individual analyst data to be stored on the PC, project data on the minicomputer and the corporate dictionary on the mainframe.

The CUSTOMISER product can be purchased or services utilized from companies who own the tool and provide a customizing service. One such resulting product is RELEASE which provides an environment within the XLD interface to move data. Input form the user end is required in order to be able to interface at a line level with the DATAMANAGER product. Use of templates for corporate dictionary input is highly recommended. Movement of data from the local to corporate dictionary should be strictly under control of the date Management Group to provide the neccessary quality assurance. The Dictionary Controller should report at a very high level. The introduction of an AI (Artificial Intelligence) knowledge co-ordinator at the mainframe corporate dictionary level will ensure consistency across the developers. All data must be co-ordinated with central information.

The templates provided are based on a logical group and data element.

RELEASE					
OPTIONS	MIGRATION	REPORTS	UTILITIES	EXIT	
FUNCTION	EXPORT	IMPORT			
	EXPORT FILE				
OLD VALUE	XXXXX.EXP				
FILE NAME					

Figure 8.3 : Example of a template.

102

With the SAA TECHNICAL ARCHITECTURE CONCEPT BASED ON DB2/SQL (or any platform methodology with relational database) the logical group-data element definition is greatly simplified and enables entities such as CUSTOMER to be held on a project local dictionary and equated to a DB2 or relational table on the logical design. This can result in a great deal of physical DB2 work at the local dictionary level and then porting this information to the corporate level. A key issue is the dictionary storing of information such as delete or insert cluster information and access paths.

Finally views and joins (all relational operations) apply to dictionaries. A view is a subset of data perceived by one person. The only fields shown are those that the user is interested in at the time. Many views are linked to provide HYPERVIEWS which is the current look at the local dictionary as seen from the central repository. Joins and other relational operations that are stored on say the DB2 catalogue should be reflected in the EXCELERATOR dictionary.

As a relational database grows larger the data dictionary grows correspondingly larger, complicated and more difficult to control. A great deal of work remains in this area.

4   STANDARDS ENFORCEMENT

Another strength of the EXCELERATOR tool is the ability to enforce standards. EXCELERATOR has a facility called QUICKSTART which enable the user to customize standards on-line as a separate project and then overlay the standards to the actual projects for help key access. While diagrams are being drawn and dictionaries updated the standards help screens are available. This enables naming standards to be indicated.

A table of codes, class list and set of keywords provide some system checking during the design process. Error detection is not fully interactive but this may be overcome by running the design and dictionaries through a microcomputer database batch run to check for discrepancies of name or ownership. A typical name for checking would be:

WBCU-CUST-CODE

where WBCU is ownership, CUST an entity and CODE a class or keyword.

The ownership code appears on the corporate dictionary and defaults on the local dictionary by customization of the EXCELERATOR dictionary to recognise ownership. The microcomputer database system such as RBASE allows application integrity rules to be applied to the EXCELERATOR dictionary.

For large systems and purchased packages writing dictionary load programs for both corporate and local dictionaries will save much time. The standards as defined in QUICKSTART can be used to audit the load process.

A weakness of QUICKSTART is the inability to produce a properly formatted manual without much difficulty.

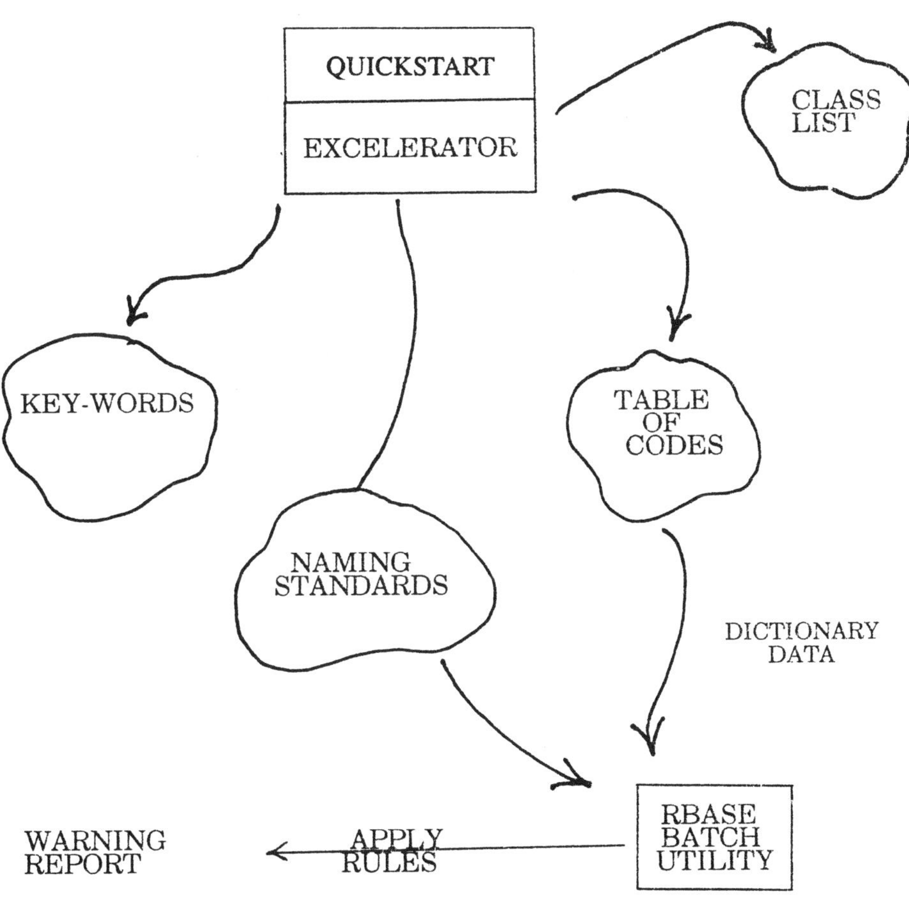

Figure 8.4 : Proper use of QUICKSTART

5   DATABASE MANAGEMENT

A weakness of EXCELERATOR is that the dictionary is small and cannot be considered as a corporate dictionary in IBM mainframe enviroments. Linking the EXCELERATOR dictionary to a microcomputer relational database gives it the properties that are lacking at present but only at a workstation and not mainframe level.

VAX environments, (DEC-only shops) should be able to utilise a corporate to local dictionary environment with sole use of the EXCELERATOR product.

The output reporting facilities of EXCELERATOR can be difficult to learn and manipulation of the dictionary by other means is often desirable. For instance, the ability to query the EXCELERATOR local dictionary using SQL. To facilitate this a data element entity list is created. This entity list is exported to an ASCII file. Using the gateway features of the RBASE database management system the file is imported to RBASE and English-like queries applied against the entity list. Any such entity list or analysis matrix can be exported easily from EXCELERATOR and further analysis matrix can be exported easily from EXCELERATOR and further analysed by relational database systems.

The author has been involved in beta test of the DB2 interface. This interface is waiting for a two-way link to the DB2 catalogue which is due to be strategic just after the 1.9 release is shipped. In the short term partial connections to the DB2 catalogue are easy to define.

An SQL query against the DB2 catalogue will produce a PDS (partitioned dataset) work-file which is duly edited to removed headers and superflous characters. An in-house COBOL program then reformats the data to EXCELERATOR format and an ASCII download process moves it to the PC. The DB2 catalogue can then be interrogated at a PC relational database level.

This interface with DB2 provides a good facility for logical to physical database design mapping. To accommodate the multi-product environment aliases are held in the EXCELERATOR dictionary at appropriate positions. The DB2 alias is always in position 3 so that physical DB2 reports can be achieved by swapping logical and physical names. The dictionary can be customized to increase the number of aliases.

The DATAMANAGER three digit code needs some handling as it is meaningless to EXCELERATOR users but provides a unique index for DATAMANAGER. The safest way to handle this is to assign a three digit code by the system and protect it on the EXCELERATOR data element alias portion of the screen. Other aliases that are required are COBOL, ADABAS, ASSEMBLER and package related names. For OLTP a link to TANDEM or SYBASE related ports is required.

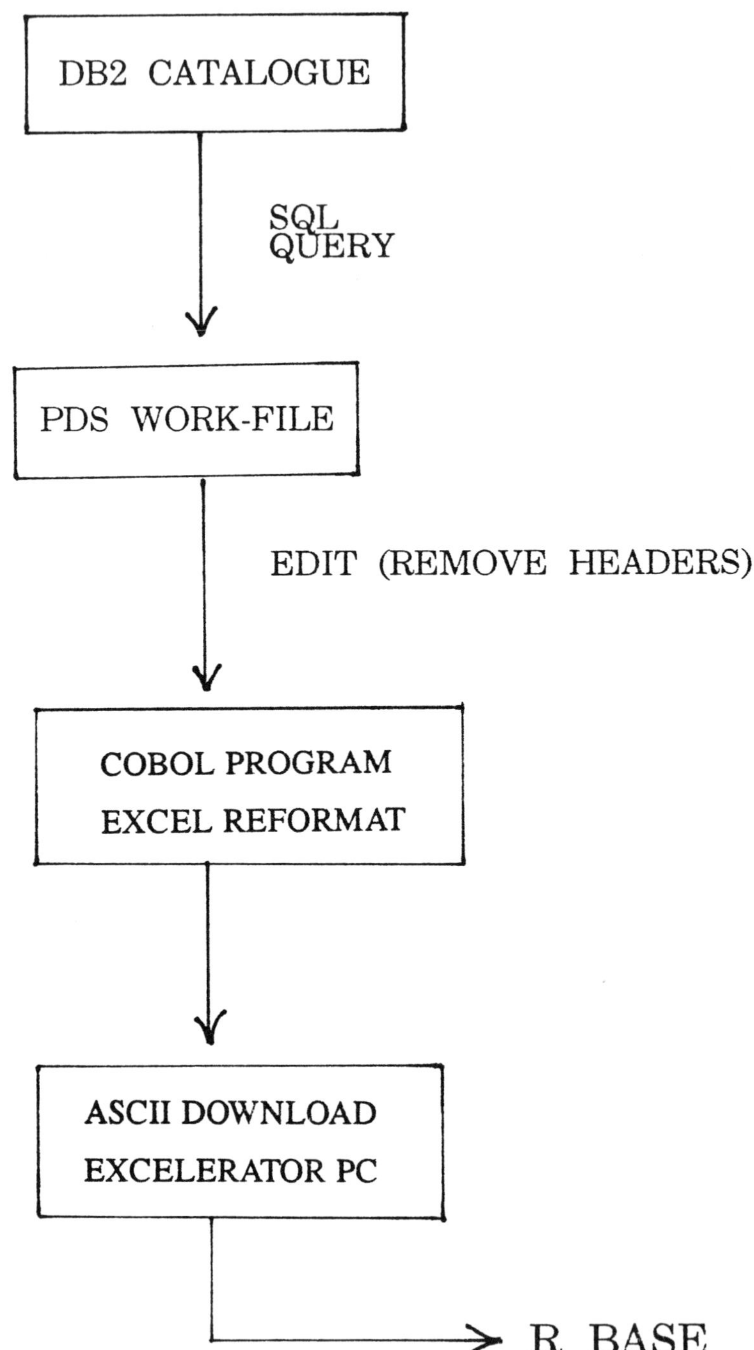

Figure 8.5 : DB2 catologue interface.

6   EXPERT SYSTEMS

A weakness of EXCELERATOR over some other analyst workbenches is the integration of AI technology e.g. PROLOG to the tool. Integration of this feature, although highly desirable, would inhibit the speed of EXCELERATOR and so has been omitted. The same is true of the lack of WINDOWS technology at present. Index Technology have gone for functionality until industry standards are more developed.

It is necessary to include intelligent rule checking when implementing logical designs for major projects. For instance in a bank linking a customer entity to an accounting entity is an acceptable link but linking the customer to a golf club entity is not. By providing object-oriented links and passing files to system software such as CRYSTAL, organizations can provide model evaluation for EXCELERATOR designs. This again is the mapping facilities that allow the links to be customized to expert systems or 4GLs such as FOCUS.

The normalization (extended analysis) feature of 1.8 can be analysed by expert systems to assess qualities of design. This provides input to the denormalization process required for DB2 physical design.

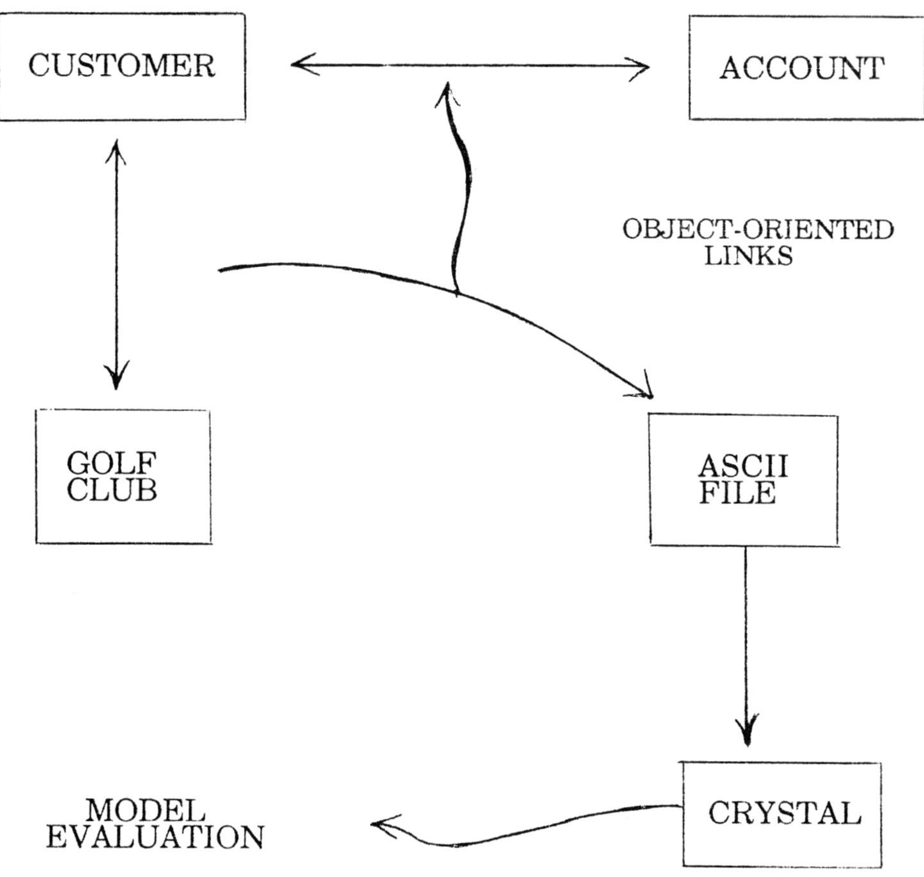

Figure 8.6 : EXCELERATOR graph.

7 SECURITY

Due to the dictionary links to the mainframe system, extra security is required for the EXCELERATOR system. Systems are available such as PROTEC, which protect the A drive, restrict DOS access and blank the screen. In addition the RBASE-EXCELERATOR control environment so defined can be protected at .EXE and .COM levels as the system is now compiled code.

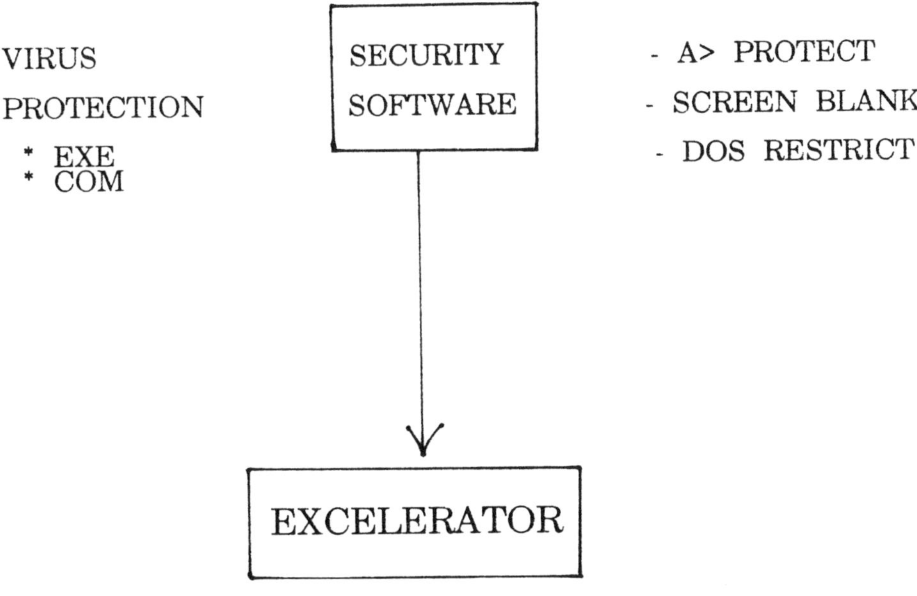

Figure 8.7 : Security — dictionary data protection to mainframe.

8   FUTURE

- I see two major factors in the future:

    1. Replacement of the corporate dictionary by an object-oriented dictionary similar to the one created by SAPIENS software. This provides messages about two-objects - records and elements. A compile button links the messages to the two objects to create a powerful corporate dictionary. The link between the EXCELERATOR dictionary and the object-oriented software can again be effected.

    2. Full strategic planning using PC-PRISM. PC-PRISM is a tool for automating the planning process. It spans strategic functional and organizational systems. It is essentially the automation of the business matrix and transfer of the relationships to EXCELERATOR.

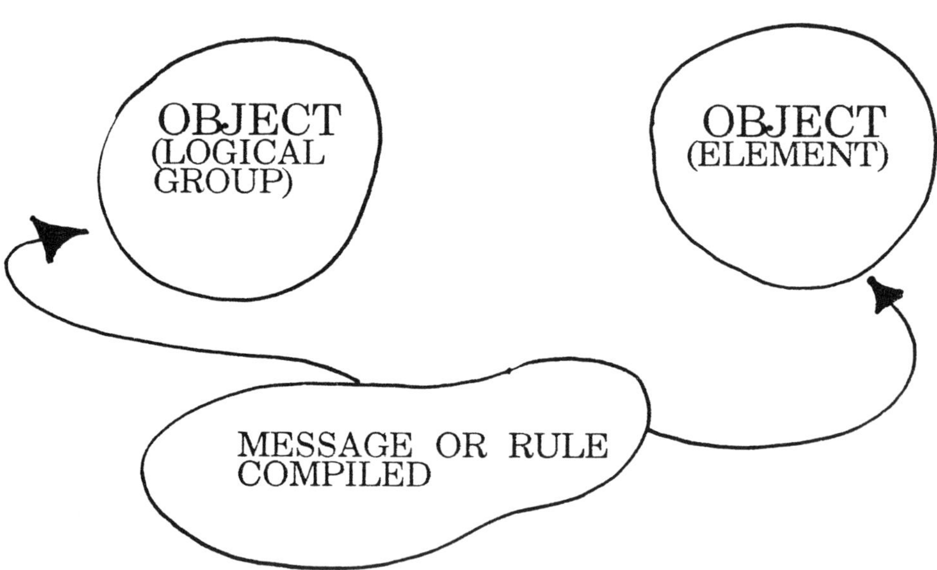

Figure 8.8 : Future — object-oriented corporate dictionary.

9
FAST DEVELOPMENT OF SYSTEMS WHICH HAVE TO ALLOW FOR CONSIDERABLE CHANGE DURING THEIR LIFE CYCLE

Gerard Lennox, CONSENSUS

This short paper is based on the author's experiences using tools to develop relatively sophisticated commercial systems where the requirements will frequently change.

There is nothing new in changing requirements during development but in these cases it was taken to extremes. Indeed, the one common characteristic of the applications was that they would constantly change during their operational life.

A further problem was that the application areas had not been computerised before, at least as far as the users were concerned.

To compound all this, the systems were unspecified in any conventional sense and they had to be operational in a very short space of time.

To make the writing of this paper even more difficult than normal, the applications must remain confidential to the clients concerned. In every case the client decided that the resulting system gave a certain competitive edge. They therefore exercised their contractual right to restrict details of the actual applications. However, they have not raised any objection to the principles being discussed.

Before getting into the meat of the paper, it is perhaps worth providing a little background to set the scene. At Consensus we have specialised in helping clients to quickly determine their requirements. Indeed, we have often helped to uncover requirements that no-one suspected were there. This is normally accomplished in a very short space of time (typically less than ten days) by employing a number of special techniques. Most of these FAST techniques involve working with the user group in a very intensive manner.

By using the FAST requirement definition process a number of things often happen. Firstly, we often become involved with very senior and forceful individuals within the user community. Such people normally have not been closely involved before with traditional mainframe developments. They often react badly to the timescales involved and the rigidity imposed on their thinking by conventional systems analysis techniques and procedures.

Secondly, and in many ways more importantly, they refuse to accept that they must pre-think and allow for every eventuality that may occur during the systems operational life. This is no more so than in the financial services area where the very act of thinking about a system often triggers new product and marketing ideas. Especially where operational life can often be defined in months rather than years.

It has been said before, but bears repeating - "in financial services the product is always the same - money". It is only the delivery vehicle that changes which, in this case, is the system.

Thirdly, we are attempting to manage the users' expectations in terms of what can be delivered as a reliable working system in a given time and budget. Again, the old truisms apply that time is more important than budget. Yet simply throwing programmers at a project is often worse than useless because the communication overhead involved negates any other productivity gain.

With this as a background it became clear that to deal with such demanding clients we must find an equally rapid method of delivering systems.

After a number of false starts with fourth-generation languages and relational databases we turned to expert systems and object-orientated programming techniques.

Like all good discoveries this came about by accident. One of the team was experimenting with a demonstration copy of some software and tucked away in the last few pages on the manual was the gem we had been looking for.

At last a solution that was normally only available on a micro but which allowed us to use the multi-user power of a mini/mainframe relational database.

At once we appeared to be in a different league. Ease of development on a micro but with the multi-user power to support several hundred simultaneous users.

But what has all this to do with CASE tools which is the theme of this series of papers?

Well, put at its most simple, we were experimenting with object-orientated techniques as a way of documenting a system design.

By extending the conventional concept of an entity model we were able to define "objects" or things of unique interest to us.

We were then able to consider what actions should be applied to the objects. In more conventional terms this would be considered the functional decomposition. The unusual thing about object-orientated systems in this case is that the objects take on characteristics. In this way much of the conventional program definition and data validation becomes redundant.

As an example simply by defining an invoice we give it an identity and limit some of the processing because it must have a unique identification and it must belong to a customer. Obvious you say but think for a moment how much system definition we have saved every time we refer to an invoice from now on.

The next gain came when we were able to separate the logic (rules) from the procedure and the associated data. We do this using a type of forms processor that handles the display and request for data. However the rules that are being applied are completely independent of the display. It is quite arbitary whether the data is displayed or not.

Finally we are able to store the resulting data in a conventional relational data base such as Ingres. This gives the multi-user capability and high volume data storage that most serious commercial applications require. As the application is delivered on a PC or workstation it is possible to have much of the processing performed in the terminal rather than in the mainframe. This dramatically reduces the cost per user and allows the application to contain many of the "user friendly" features of workstations.

So what has this to do with rapid change? Well, the answer is quite a lot. By decoupling the logic and the display we simply have to change the rules and we have a different application.

Take a simple insurance example.

- Normal male
- if yes
- Does he drink
- if yes
- how old
- read
- rates table
- calculate quote by age x rate x drink factor

However if we now decide that we should ask if he is married we would normally have to change our data structures and our screen layouts. Not so with this approach. Simply by putting in a new rule a new question is asked of the operator and the calculation is altered.

In this way we are able to deal with completely unthought of requirements at the drop of a hat. Often changing every workstation's version of the application overnight as a by product of automatically down loading data from a central mainframe.

The key to this is the ability to specify "objects" define logical rules and handle the human interface requirements as separate issues.

Over all the productivity gains have been substantial as well as providing properly documented systems written in English like pseudo code that are extremely quick and safe to enhance as time goes on.

10

USE OF DESIGNAID
WITHIN HOSKYNS GROUP

Bob Grover
Principal Consultant
and
Cally Ware
Product Manager
CASE and Productivity Tools Division, Hoskyns Group plc

1   HOSKYNS USE OF DESIGNAID

Hoskyns Group comprises over 3000 people, in various specialist groups-by application speciality (e.g. Financial, Manufacturing) or by development environment (IBM mainframe, IBM mid-range, ICL, HP, DEC) or by business orientation (Facilities Management, Professional Services).

Each part of the Group has its own development specialisms. DesignAid is starting to be used by most parts of the Group for conventional team-based development using structured analysis, and for several other less obvious uses.

This chapter describes the current practical experiences and plans in several areas which involve not-so-conventional uses of an analyst workbench. These are:

- CCS - London Residuary Body

    - "DesignAid as a help to staying in business"

- Facilities Management

    - "DesignAid for better documentation and designs"

    - "DesignAid for Operational Run Sheets etc"

- Methodologies and CASE

  – "Using DesignAid for Deliverables Creation and Management"

- Systems Analyst Education

- Modular Development Methodology

  – "DesignAid as an analyst front-end to a 4GL system"

- CUTAS

  – "Reverse Engineering with DesignAid"

2   CCS - THE LONDON RESIDUARY BODY COMPUTING COMPANY

In mid-1987, the GLC Computing Services were taken over by Hoskyns as a facilities management contract, and were set up as a new company called CCS. This group comprises about 120 CS&P people. Their individual responsibilities are spread widely, and no specific distinctions into analysts and programmers as such are made.

CCS have been looking at the need for CASE tools, in particular analyst workbenches, for eighteen months. The main drive that was pushing them in that direction was the need to continue to be able to win business in the future. In particular this means the ability to produce designs which are easy to update, and are mechanically cross checked for completeness. CCS see these abilities as essential to their survival and growth plans.

A three person study team has been evaluating the specific needs for CASE tools, and setting out a plan for implementation and sucessful use.

Early in 1989, an initial 12 copies of DesignAid have been bought and were being installed during the second quarter of 1989. They will be used by approximately 30 people within CCS, for the development of new systems in a reasonably conventional structured analysis environment.

CCS have set up a specific training program to ensure that all their people use similar forms of structured analysis, and will be using the tools in the same ways. This involves refresher training for the structured analysis techniques, and specific tool training to ensure that the locally developed standards and templates for examples fo structured analysis constructs are being used consistently and are known about by all the users.

It is an interesting development, because it is from a business point of view, essentially a defensive position, that says "We have to recognize our need for tools for design support in order to stay in business".

3   FACILITIES MANAGMENT SITE

One of Hoskyns FM sites, which started with 30 people in development and has now grown to 60 people in development, has been using DesignAid since late 1988. This site provides the full FM facility: Hoskyns is contracted to run and maintain existing systems, and develop new systems, for several clients, based around one (enhanced) computer installation.

They started with one copy, to use on a major feasibility study for the client on that site, but also to evaluate its usefulness for support of development and all their other jobs in general.

The feasibility study has been a great success. The use of DesignAid has assisted the development group in presenting clear dataflow diagrams and professional documentation to enable the client to make their decisions more easily. The project under consideration is going to be 20-25 man years and will involve 15 people and will require many more copies of DesignAid as the project proceeds.

3.1 Methodology implications

In fact this site started by putting a more formal methodology into operation, in order to reduce the risks of new systems development. As a result of the phase structure of the methodology, the development people have been able to make a better case for using the analyst workbench and other tools during even the initial stages of the project. They believe that without the methodology, they would not have had the confidence to invest the money in the analyst workbench. They would have gone ahead in the traditional way and spent a lot of paper writing and re-writing proposals. In fact the use of the methodology and DesignAid have re-inforced each other; the documentation facilities of DesignAid have been extensively used to make the methodology more attractive, and the methodology has provided the list of deliverables that make up the documentation itself.

3.2 Operational documentation

This site has recently taken on board the work of another large mainframe, from a different FM client location (after all this is what facitlities management is all about!). This new work did not arrive very well documented, from an operational point of view, so DesignAid was being used to produce operational documentation, including system run charts, system flow charts, and operation run schedules. This uses the graphic capabilities of DesignAid and the ability to annotate pictures with text comments. Nobody on the site expected DesignAid to be used for this purpose; but having it available has proved extremely valuable. In fact the site is planning to make DesignAid the standard documentation tool for all operational run schedules etc throughout.

3.3 Training

In order to achieve successful implementation of DesignAid, and to make more people aware of what is available, two training courses have been run for initially 18 people. Of the 27 PCs already on site, 9 have been used on these training courses, so that each person uses his or her own PC full time during the training.

3.4 View of product

The local manager summarizes his view as follows: "Now that we have got used to the methodology and the DesignAid features, we can see that they support each other very thoroughly. Without the methodology we would have been harder to convince about the use of the tool; without the tool it would have been harder to introduce and encourage people to use the methodology and produce the documentation to fully professional standards. In fact, I now look on DesignAid as the equivalent for a systems analyst of a word processor for a secretary: it's hard to imagine surviving without using it. The tool "makes it easy" for the analyst to do a better job".

4   METHODOLOGIES AND CASE

In a recent copy of Corporate Computing, a dozen leading CASE suppliers were asked a standard set of questions about the take up of CASE tools. Virtually everyone talked positively about methodologies as very helpful to the successful use of CASE tools. It seems that now the tools are actually available, "methodology" has stopped being a dirty word!

Hoskyns, "Methods Division" are developing their existing range of methodologies to provide mechanical assistancr in implementation and use, via DesignAid and its sister product, Life Cycle Manager.

The combination of these tools and the appropriate methodology for the project provides a completely new level of machine assistance to the working development team. For example, analysts can call up (and copy directly into their documentation and designs) sample dataflow diagrams or entity models, or can ask for guidance and example, from the on-line methodology, held on disk. This cuts down the learning and support effort of the methodology implementation, and ensures that the latest information and examples are available to all people.

Life Cycle Manager is essentially a Deliverables Management system, which tracks the elements of documentation (deliverables) from the point where a deliverable is created, through the QA review process, to the point where a deliverable is used as input to a later activity. Deliverables Management is linked to progress reviews automatically, so the project manager and the team members all know what is going on, and where it has got to. LCM uses a deliverables matrix to tune and validate the project structure.

This system is now released in the UK as Hoskyns' PROWESS. It is the only mechanically assisted methodology range available, and it depends on using the DesignAid workbench as the basic document handling and modification system inside it.

4.1 Modular development methodology

Hoskyns MDM is a way of building systems very quickly and effectively using MUMPS as the development environment. This system was originally developed on Digital machines, but is now available widely on mini computers and PCs.

Hoskyns MDM contains a large number of tools and techniques for building screens and reports, and the processing code that links them, very quickly. It is effectively a fourth-generation development system.

This division of Hoskyns is using DesignAid for the systems analysis work, and then passing the dictionary of objects created during systems analysis, on through an interface program, into the MDM environment. This makes systems analysis link into development much more easily, and the programs across the interface create the vast majority of the MDM full dictionaries directly. This speeds up the overall system development process dramatically.

4.2 Systems analyst education

Hoskyns, Education Division runs very high quality professional training courses, for systems analysts among others. This includes a four week systems analysis course, and specialist courses on structured anslysis, data analysis, etc. These courses are intended to be tool independent, of course. Because the vast majority of ansalysts do not have access to these tools, yet!

DesignAid is demonstrated on these courses as an example of how mechanical checking can remove the drudgery of doing the same checking by hand. The point is made very clearly that manual checking is possible, but machine checking is much easier and much more complete! Documentation maintenance and creation is also covered, but again only after people have been trained to do it all with pencils and erasers in the normal way.

These courses are not saying that DesignAid is the only answer, they are using it as an example of a workbench.

5   CUTAS, REVERSE ENGINEERING IN PRACTICE

Hoskyns' Financial Systems Division (FSD) has used the Hoskyns DesignAid analyst workbench to reverse engineer a fully documented design of its successful Computerised Unit Trust Administration System (CUTAS). This Unit Trust Blueprint is available on DesignAid files so that users can tailor it interactively to their own business and computing environments.

CUTAS was first released on IBM mid-range System/3X machines in 1982. Since then, this version has been continuously updated and enhanced, meeting all current legislative requirements for its more than 40 users in the UK, Channel Islands and Luxembourg. DesignAid was introduced last year to help its strong market position grow and extend.

"CUTAS has evolved from a system implemented before the availability of Computer-Aided Software Engineering (CASE) tools like analysts workbenches," explains Steve Webb, Director of Hoskyns' FSD. "Although this was perfectly acceptable for the development of the original package in the original environment, we needed to build a structured design to help us broaden its customer base.

"The Blueprint concept supported by DesignAid is a major advance in our ability to port CUTAS to different systems and to adapt it quickly to keep pace with new technologiew, such as the IBM AS/400 range and SAA standards," Webb says.

"It provides a flexible design created from a proven working system. Changes are made at the design level — before code is produced. This is inherently more reliable than traditional techniques.

"The resultant Blueprint solutions combine the robustness of a standard package with the efficiency of customised software. This also helps to meet the growing demand from companies for products that fit their overall Information System Strategy, for example by integration with corporate client databases and distributed processing capabilities."

CUTAS consists of a number of modules, of which Dealing Registration and Savings Accounts are the most widely used. The Unit Trust Blueprint is also available as individual modules or a complete system; its cost, including a copy of Designaid, starts at about £40,000 for the Dealing module.

Part Three

New Directions and Developments

11

THE DISTRIBUTED DEVELOPMENT ENVIRONMENT:
WHERE ARE CASE TOOLS MOVING IN THE NEAR FUTURE?

Simon Holloway
Principal Consultant, DCE Information Management Consultancy Ltd

1   INTRODUCTION

In the last 5 years, we have seen a major software revolution in the form of tools to help speed up the application development life cycle. CASE tools, in all their forms, are changing the way IT develop and produce applications. This paper first of all looks at the current situations with CASE technology and identifies the current problems. It then looks at the requirements of Second-Generation CASE technology based on the need to support the "distributed development environment".

2   CASE PRODUCTS

CASE is an acronym of Computer Aided Software Engineering, a term which is rather vague and can be applied to almost any product. There are almost as many definitions as there are products. In an article in ICP Business Software review in December 1987[1], three categories of CASE products were put forward:

- Front-end CASE tools - these support the belief that the need is for a productivity aid to help design the document systems, leaving the programming function to the language most suited to the application. These are commonly referred to in the literature as Analyst Workbench products.

- Back-end CASE tools - these support the belief that true productivity gains come when the systems design is automatically converted into efficient code in such a manner that it can be easily maintained. These are often referred to as System Generators, but this category also can be viewed as including Fourth-Generation Languages, as they provide the same facilities.

- Life-cycle products - these address both the aforementioned activities. These products are tied in to James Martin's masterplan for information engineering. The life-cycle approach to software design and construction is the ultimate dream for many software developers. Figure 11.1 shows examples.

LIFE-CYCLE PRODUCTS

PRODUCT	DISTRIBUTOR	HARDWARE
CORVISION	CORTEX	DEC VAX, DEC PC & IBM PC
ADS	DELTA SOFTWARE	IBM M/F, ICL M/F, DEC VAX&IBM PC
APS	SOFTWARE GENERATORS	IBM M/F &PC
IEW	ARTHUR YOUNG	IBM M/F & PC
IEF	JMA	IBM M/F & PC

Figure 11.1 : Examples of life - cycle CASE tools.

In addition, there are two other major categories of CASE tools:

- Integrated Project Support Environment (IPSE) tools - An IPSE can be viewed as a CASE tool within a common environment, which offers an integrated total system development environment.

- Information Resource Planning tools - These tools provide support for the planning and high level control of the information resource. They provide the means to derive the required information systems from the objectives and critical success factors of an organization.

2.1 Front-end CASE tools (analyst workbenches)

A spate of products have appeared since 1985. These products support systems analysts in precisely documenting the business requirements. They support the latest methodologies for systems analysis. The methods and the products rely heavily on graphics. Typically these products provide a graphics interface to allow a systems analyst to draw diagrams to represent the results of his work. Different kinds of diagrams are supported according to the methods supported by the vendor. Dataflow diagrams are provided by most products. Data model diagrams are provided by almost as many. Various kinds of activity model are common. In addition, most products have weak data dictionary facilities, with attractive pop up screen formats to fill in. Often these screen formats are closely linked to the diagram. Reporting facilities are in general fairly limited at present. Figure 11.2 below shows a list of products within this category.

FRONT-END/UPPER CASE PRODUCTS

PRODUCT	DISTRIBUTOR	HARDWARE
DATA MODELLER	ANALYST WORKBENCH PRODUCTS	APPLE MACINTOCHES
TOOLKIT	YOURDON	IBM PC
DESIGN MATTER	ICL	ICL M/F & DRS 3000
PAGE	INFOREM	IBM PC
SPEEDBUILDER	JACKSON SYSTEM	IBM PC
MANAGERVIEW	MSP	IBM M/F &PC
EXCELERATOR	EXCELERATOR SOFTWARE	IBM PC
DEPICTOR	CA	IBM M/F &PC
AUTOMATE PLUS	LBMS	IBM PC
PROKIT*WORKBENCH	MCDONNELL DOUGLAS	IBM PC
DEFT	KERNEL	APPLE MACINTOSHES
SYSTEM FACTORY	SYSTEMATICA	SUN UNIX
CASE*DESIGNER	ORACLE	SUN UNIX
FOUNDATION	ARTHUR ANDERSON	IBM PC &M/F

Figure 11.2 : Examples of front-end CASE tools.

2.2 Back-end CASE tools (system generators and application development tools)

System generators take the results of analysis and automatically design screens, logic and database structures from which a working complete application can be generated. These products have the potential to completely alter the process used to build many commercial applications. Such products will take the business data model and apply rules to design database structures for a specified database. The model of business activities will be used to generate application logic in COBOL or possibly other languages. These tools build in design rules, thus reducing the amount of time and the level of knowledge that the application developer needs. In addition, generation across different hardware environments would be no more difficult, opening up the possibility of a new level of hardware and operating system independence.

There are many application development tools on the market that replace some or all of the functionality of COBOL and give major productivity gains for application development. Examples of such products are Cincom's MANTIS, Software AG's Natural and DEC's Rally. At present these products are selling heavily. They are making a major impact on development costs. However, they do not tackle the problems of assisting the systems analyst and their total contribution to solving the application development problem is thus limited. Some of the products of this type have analyst's workbench and system generation facilities added to them. ICL and Computer Associates are examples of vendors going in this direction. Cullinet is another, having acquired marketing rights to AUTO-MATE. Other products that do not follow this trend are likely to become obsolete.

Figure 11.3 shows examples of this type of CASE tool.

BACK-END/LOWER CASE PRODUCTS

PRODUCT	DISTRIBUTOR	HARDWARE
GENER/OL	PANSOPHIC	IBM M/F & PC
TELON	PANSOPHIC	IBM M/F & PC
INTELAGEN	ON-LINE	IBM M/F
KNOWLEDGE BUILD	CULLINET	DEC VAZ
IDEAL	CA	IBM M/F
IDEAL-ESCORT	CA	IBM PC
MANTIS	CINCOM	IBM, DEC , ICL
NATURAL	SOFTWARE AG	IBM, DEC, WANG, SIEMENS
ADS	CULLINET	IBM M/F
POWERHOUSE	COGNOS	DEC VAX
RAPID-GEN	RAPID-GEN SYSTEMS	DEC VAX
QUICKBUILD	ICL	ICL
RALLY	DIGITAL	DEC VAX

Figure 11.3 : Examples of back-end CASE tools.

2.3 Integrated Project Support Environment tools (IPSEs)

There are two main approaches to IPSEs, Open and Closed. An Open IPSE provides a framework within which each project can integrate the tools most suited to its needs, irrespective of whether they come from the IPSE supplier, another supplier or from in-house. A Closed IPSE offers a package of design, project management, data handling methodologies and CASE tools that must be applied by all projects using it.

There are only four main IPSEs available in the UK:

- ISTAR from Imperial Software Technology;

- BIS/IPSE from BIS;

- GENOS from GEC;

- MAESTRO from Softlab/Philips

2.4 Information Resource Planning tools

With the growth of acceptance of the need to properly plan the development of Information Systems, so as to link their development to corporate objectives, a need has arisen for a set of tools to support this process. These tools have been developed in the main by particular methodology vendors to support their own particular brand of Information Resource Planning.

Figure 11.4 shows examples of this type of CASE tool.

TOOLS TO SUPPORT INFORMATION RESOURCE PLANNING

PRODUCT	DISTRIBUTOR	HARDWARE
SUPER-MATE	LBMS	IBM PC
PC PRISM	EXCELERATOR SOFTWARE	IBM PC
INFORMATION PLANNER	ARTHUR YOUNG	IBM PC
DAWN	4S BUSINESS TECHNOLOGY	IBM PC
TETRARCH	PA	IBM M/F & PC
ENTELLECT	ENTELLECT/CONSENSUS	IBM PC

Figure 11.4 : Examples of IRP CASE tools.

3 CASE TOOL SUPPORT OF THE APPLICATION LIFE-CYCLE

CASE tools offer the first major automation of the analysis and design process of systems building. The increasing demand from end users for new systems and the skills shortfall is driving CASE tool designers to support the complete application development life-cycle. I believe that such tools will provide the productivity and quality gains needed.

This begs the question, what is the complete application development life-cycle that is needed to be supported. Figure 11.5 shows my idea of the sort of structured development life-cycle that needs to be supported. The figure also related this to the UK governments' SSADM methods phases.

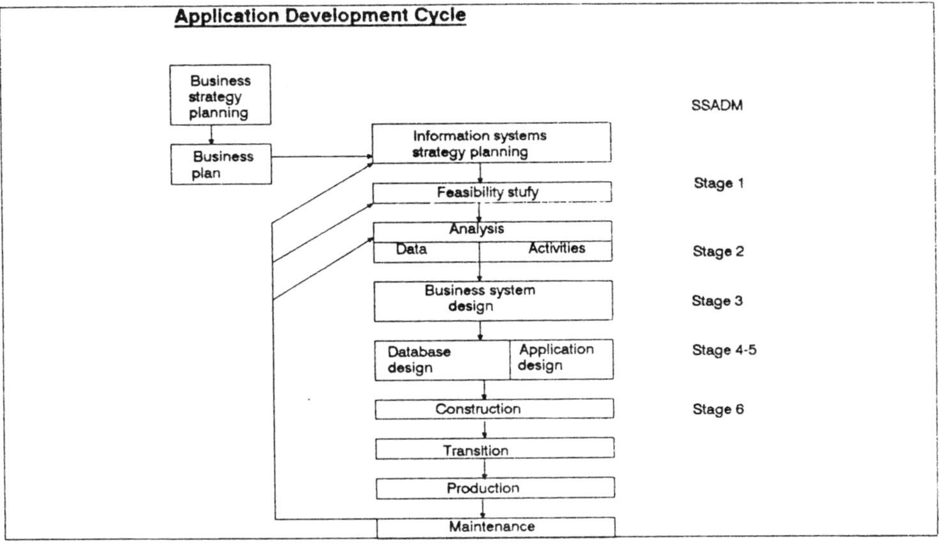

Figure 11.5 : Application development life-cycle.

Figure 11.6 shows for a sample of current CASE tools, the support given to the application development life-cycle.

This shows one of the major current shortfalls of current CASE tools, full support for the application development life-cycle is not there.

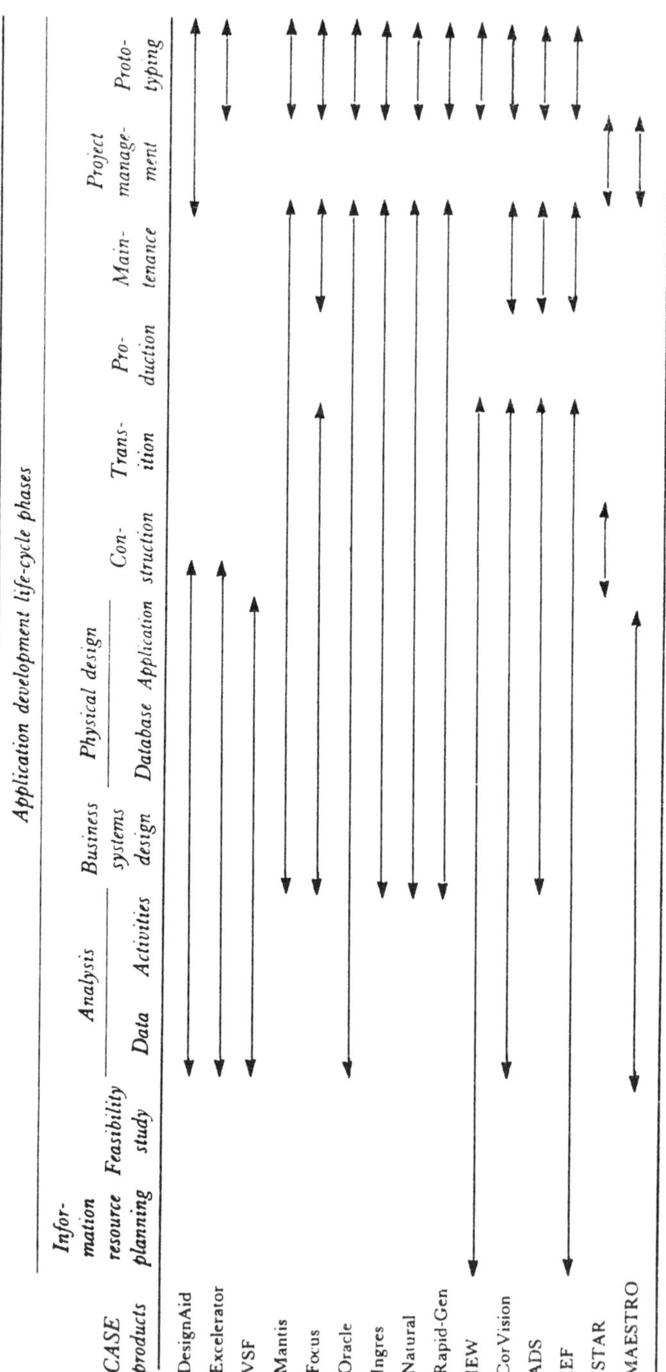

Figure 11.6 : Summary of application development life-cycle support provided by products reviewed.

134

A key innovation is the development of more precise notations that can be used consistently to capture and subsequently detail analysis and design specifications. This brings some aspects of formal methods to commercial systems development. This notation is often graphical as this is the most natural and understandable way of describing complex systems. These new notations and methods are supported by CASE tools and indeed these improvements to methods are only practical with machine support. The combination of better tools and methods improve the reliability, efficiency and speed with which systems are developed. Some CASE tools now include capabilities for code generation and the creation and testing of prototypes.

The next major step in CASE tool development will be the application of artificial intelligence (AI) to the development process. AI systems will embody the principles of good system design. They will come to contain the kind of knowledge and expertise gleaned by software developers over many years, and thus further tackle the skill shortages problem. I expect that expert CASE tools will support the developers by providing an advising facility to a developer when he is faced with a problem.

4   CURRENT PROBLEMS

There are a number of problems with the current products that must by solved during the next three years:

- Current PCs as workstations are not powerful enough;

- A central data dictionary is required in a distributed development environment;

- Facilities to booking in and out groups of definitions in a controlled manner are needed;

- Version control;

- The generation of code for foreign environments.

4.1 PCs as workstations

The CASE vendors, and in particular the back-end CASE vendors, where support for multiple target environments is part of the package, view the PC as the development platform hardware of the future. They see a time in the short term, when analysts and designers will have their own PC, rather than a dumb terminal. This is confirmed by the policies of our clients.

Front-end CASE tools, such as Excelerator have exploited the graphics facilities available in the PC to provide the analyst with the means of drawing diagrams whilst still providing text handling through word processing facilities. Until recently, these sorts of tools were written to run on IBM or IBM plug compatible PCs. The PC was selected for the reasons of cost, graphics, simplicity and availability.

The amount of power available in a micro is an important factor in its usability and acceptability to an analyst. A CASE tool must be significantly faster then a paper and pencil even for initial entry of information. Current PCs only just provide an acceptable level of power at a price that is, subjectively, a little bit high for the average DP manager to buy one per analyst.

Primarily due to the graphics requirement, but also because of the complexity of the meta model, any machine on which a CASE tool resides requires considerable processing power in PC terms. Generally an "ordinary" PC is not sufficient. It needs to have a high resolution screen, high resolution printers and plotters, and considerable boosted power.

Machines such as the Apple Macintosh II and the Xerox 6085 already have very high resolution 19 inch screens and an "expensive word processor". It can be expected that rapid strides in the direction of generally available high resolution screens with enough CPU power to drive them, and sufficient disc (say 100 Mbytes) per analyst all at a reasonable price, will be seen. Japanese pressure is likely to drive the price of Sun workstations down to those of Apple Macintoshes and thus expand the workstation market still further.

Also of importance to the analyst is the availability of cheap, quiet, high resolution printers. The advent of laser printers and desk publishing software makes this a reality.

4.2 The need for a Central Data Dictionary in a Distributed Development Environment

A project is normally worked on by more than one analyst. An analyst can work on more than one project. Projects may have their own set of activities, but they will undoubtedly share data with other projects - for example a pay-roll application will use personnel data and pay data, as will the pensions application. The hardware and software configuration must allow this form of working. There is a need to share and co-ordinate information across a team. In addition, with data being recognized as a major resource, many companies have set up a data administration group, who are responsible for the corporate data. This data administration group will also need to be able to review the check work being done by development teams.

Thus, an environment where there are many dictionaries which wish to exchange information is born.

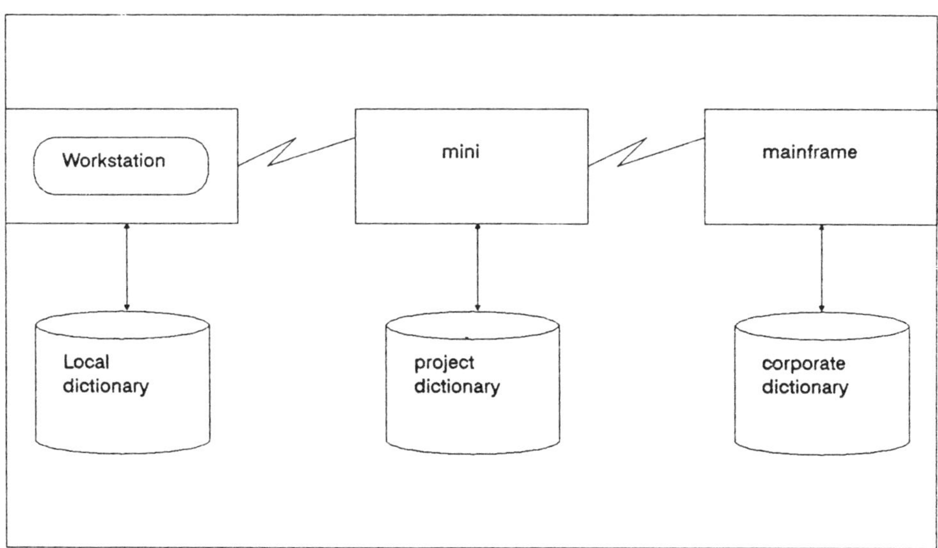

Figure11. 7 : Multi-level dictionary environment.

To provide an environment where information can be shared between distributed users, is more difficult then it first appears. It has been realized by users, as well as vendors, that CASE tools on their own are not the full answer. The CASE tool is part of an integrated set of software that includes, at a minimum, the following:

- Database Management System — to allow applications to share data;

- Data Dictionary System — to allow automated control and documentation of the data and the processes that use the data;

- Fourth-Generation System — to allow for more rapid application development;

- Query Language — to allow end users direct access to the data resource.

The key, underlying software component is the data dictionary system. Everything in the new development environment hinges on the dictionary, even though data dictionary software in itself has little changed, the other software components are now providing the user-friendly front-end that hides the dictionary from the user. The task of maintenance of dictionary objects is being automated by these other tools communicating directly with the data dictionary. CASE tools are no exception; to allow meta-information to be shared CASE tools must communicate with a central dictionary. Thus CASE tools should be viewed as a graphics and text handling front-end to dictionaries and nothing more. Figure 8 shows an example of a simple distributed development environment.

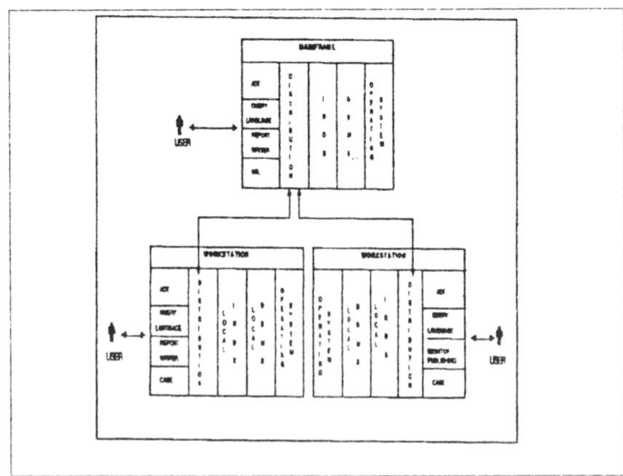

Figure 11.8 : The distributed development environment.

4.3 The booking in and out problem

The ideal is to have a centrally held database of the dictionary and diagrams, but distributed functions to powerful PCs with their own (possibly shared) graphics plotters and printers.

In this case the software must be multi-user and have good recovery, locking, consistency and integrity features. It also needs in-built "privacy" locks. When an analyst is working on a subset of data, the data is locked against update. Access to look is allowed, but a warning is issued.

A configuration, which achieves the same objective, but with reduced line activity, would be one where every workbench has its own local dictionary which is generated from the central project dictionary for the analyst to work on, and then booked back when he has finished. Unfortunately, this form of architecture is much more complex to construct. The software required to book out and transfer back is complex. Booking out is much the same as that for the previous configuration- the subset of data is locked whilst it is being worked on and retrieved access is allowed but a warning is given.

The transfer back is more difficult as update can only be achieved by comparison with the old version. To do this versions must be held, and a thorough set of change control procedures is needed.

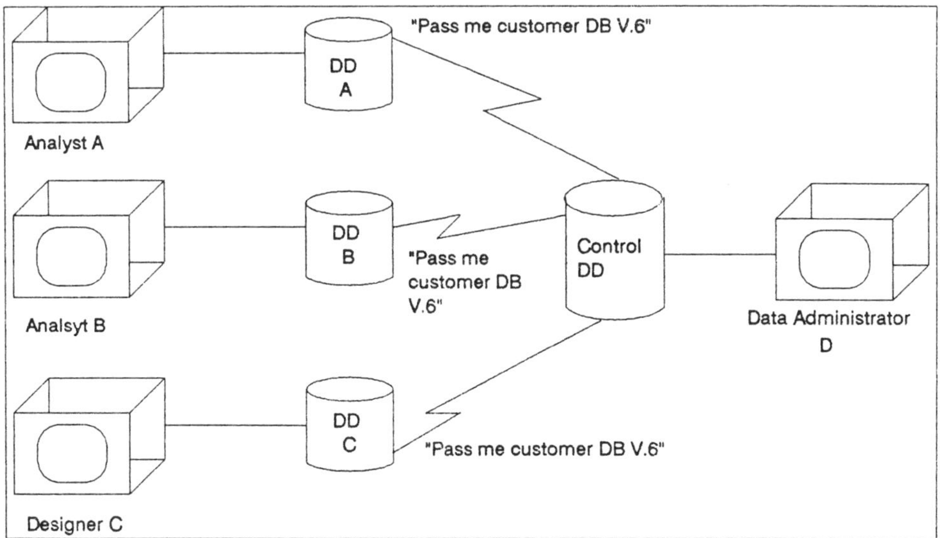

Figure 11.9 : The booking in /booking out problem.

In the short term, CASE vendors are supporting a simple export/import facility. A good example of this is the facilities provided by McDonnell Douglas's Prokit*Workbench. In the medium term, the data dictionary will control multiple versions over multiple machines. Already Inforem's PAGE product has done this. Additionally in the middle term, there is a move towards concurrent updates being handled using a server. Cortex's CorVision and Hoskyn's DesignAid are products that already support the multi-user environment. In the case of the former, this is done through close coupling of a PC and a VAX. In the long term, I see that an international standard will be in place for distributed data dictionaries.

4.4 Version control

During the systems development life-cycle a number of versions of dictionary objects will occur. The problem is further complicated when there are multiple copies of the definitions held in a distributed development environment.

The current dictionary facilities are fairly limited and do not cater for user extensions. Many front-end CASE tools have little or no version management. The users require the ability to control the change control process using the data dictionary. To be able to do this effectively, the dictionary vendors need to supply improved version management systems, that support not only version numbers, but also statuses that can be adapted to a particular site's needs. In addition, there is a need to support collections of dictionary objects, which could be based upon project needs.

Work that has been done on configuration mangement, particularly in the UNIX environment, has not been integrated with the mainstream data dictionary thinking. One of the problems is that a data dictionary holds fine granularity information, with many relationships. It is not clear in a data dictionary whether the configuration item should be at the level of a single data item definition or at the level of all definitions for a particular phase of a project. In the Portable Common Tools Environment (PCTE), the configuration item is a unit of source code. In a data dictionary this would represent many different objects with a structure between them.

The BSI IRDS panel are currently developing specifications for a full version control system for submission to ISO. Figure 11.10[3] shows the data model that has been proposed.

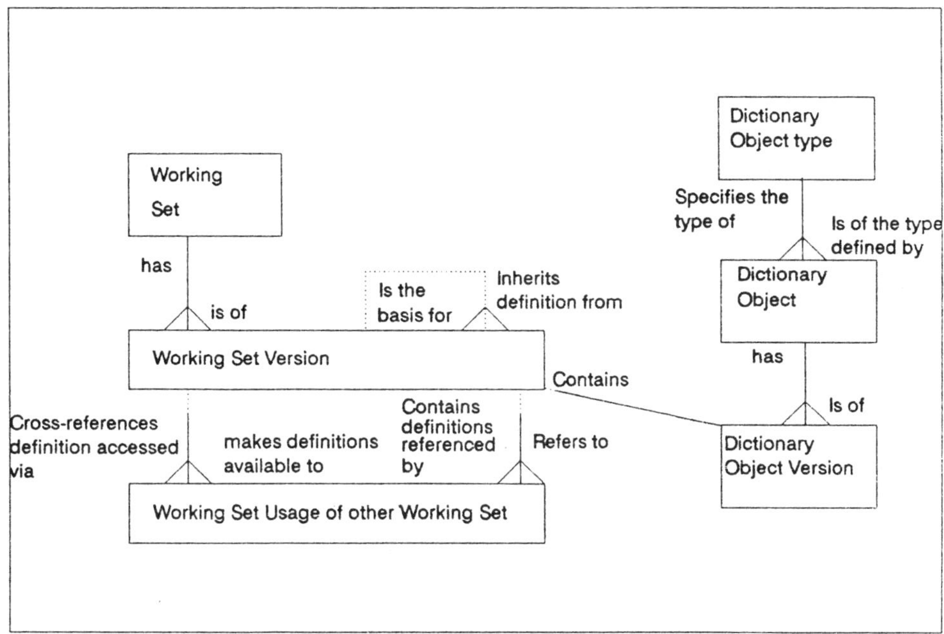

Figure 11.10 : A meta-model for version control.

4.5 The Generation Code for a foreign environment

If a user is going to use a different environment to develop in from that which the live system will run in, he needs software that shields him from the underlying operating system at least and also from TP monitor and/or time sharing system. Even with the IBM environment, the user needs to be hidden from the differences between the three IBM operation systems of DOS, VM and MVS and the two main TP monitors of IMS/DC and CICS.

4.5.1 IBM CASE vendors

Many IBM-based back-end CASE tools such as Information Builders' Focus, Software AG's Natural and Computer Associates IDEAL already shield the developer from the underlying IBM operating system. This capability has been further enhanced by carrying this down to the PC, so that application can be developed on the PC to be run on the mainframe.

Computer Associates have recently confirmed that they are working on a version of IDEAL that will run under Digital VAX VMS and UNIX operating systems. A second Applied Data Research product-Depictor, their front-end CASE tool, will also be engineered to be available in VMS and UNIX environment. This is a significant step for what has always been a "true-blue" third-party vendor.

Software AG released a mainframe CASE front-end tool to their data dictionary called PREDICT-CASE at the end of 1988. At the same time Software AG are going to bring out a VAX CASE product that uses Apple Mackintoshes as the graphic front-end to a VAX-based dictionary server. Software AG's Natural and Adabas product have been able to be used on Digital and IBM equipment for some time.

Cincom have in 1988 put together a strategy for CASE by linking to a number of independent CASE products. This CASE alliance program has seen MANTIS linked to the following:

- Aion Corporation's Aion Development system - a software environment for building inference-based DP applications for IBM;

- D. Appleton Company Inc.'s IDEF/LEVERAGE - a software system that supports structured methods and project planning;

- Index Technology Corporation's Excelerator.

Cincom's products themselves run on both Digital and IBM hardware.

4.5.2 Digital CASE vendors

Up until 1988, new Digital-based CASE tools, with the notable exception of Oracle, Ingres and Informix have not provided portability to IBM environment.

That changed last year, with Rapid-Gen, today 4GL and PRO-IV all announcing moves to run in the IBM environment.

4.5.3 The problems of incompatibility

In a recent piece of work that I did for a hardware/software vendor, I discovered that for all the claims made by vendors of complete compatibility across various operating environments, there were a number of variations. For instance, Focus running on IBM mainframes and PCs has different capabilities to the DEC version. In the MANTIS environment, the DEC version allows for the exploitation of VAX utilities from within the product. Oracle in a technical bulletin published during last quarter of 1988 produced a detailed set of guidelines to follow when designing for portability. They specifically focus on the migration of applications between asynchronous systems, such as PCs, VAX's and UNIX synchronous systems such as IBM's VM and MVS.

One way in which this problem is being looked at is the concept of Open Distributed Processing (ODP). The aim of ODP is to allow a developer to write applications for a standard distributed operating system. Such an operating system would be supported by each processor in the network. Software tools and protocols are under-developed by ANSA.IBM's Systems Applications Architecture (SAA)can be viewed as one of the first commercial ODP products.

5 THE DISTRIBUTED DEVELOPMENT ENVIRONMENT

In section 4.2, I introduced the concept of the distributed development environment, as the environment that CASE technology is pushing IT towards to adequately support the development of information systems. Are there any existing guidelines that we might be able to use to implement this environment? The answer is yes. Chris Date [4] has provided a set of rules for live distributed databases. These 12 rules plus the Fundamental Principle provide a framework.

CASE and data dictionaries links are a special type of distributed processing, and not all the rules are completely appropriate. There is a strong case for a central dictionary, to which the CASE workbenches are closely coupled. Additional rules governing the booking in and out of information from the central development dictionary are required. Outlined in the sections below are my thoughts on the applicability of these rules to the distributed development environment.

5.1 The Fundamental Principle

This is correct from the point of view of being able to access the data. The question to be asked of Meta data - is whether it is partitioned, replicated and/or fragmented? The extraction process must hide from the user where the data is physically located, and do the retrieval in the optimum manner. If a distributed data dictionary is like any other distributed database, the extraction process can be done in the same way as for the latter.

5.2 The Local Autonomy Rule

This is not completely true in the linked workstation environment, where other sites must have an appreciation of what is being worked upon at another site. Rules are needed to cover the booking in and out of meta-objects. Whent a booked out object is selected by a developer, he/she needs to know who is currently working on that item, and how long they have been working on it. So in the distributed development environment, there is a need to know what other sites are doing for certain successful operations to be done.

5.3 No Reliance on a Central Site Rule

This is definitely false; there is a definite requirement for a central data dictionary to control all the developments on the many workstations and to be used to interchange information. Thus a global data dictionary would appear to be the solution rather than a distributed one. The CASE workbenches could hold replicated parts of the global data dictionary.

5.4 Continuous Operations Rule

This is a requirement for the workstation environment. This is even true when the node containing the central dictionary is out. The workstations must be able to continue to work up to the point where an exchange of information is required.

5.5 Location Independence Rule

This is affected to a degree by the thoughts on Rules 1(see 5.2) and 2(see 5.3). A developer at a workstation needs to be aware that certain data is stored at the central dictionary, and that sometimes that data might be booked out to another developer.

5.6 Fragmentation Independence and Replication Rules

These are affected to a degree by the thoughts on Local Autonomy and no reliance on a central site. The meta data must be allowed to be fragmented and/or replicated, but there is a need to know where the data is for control purposes.

5.7 Distributed Query Processing

This is a requirement for the distributed development environment. Each developer should have their own view of the central dictionary and may have particular integrity constraints applied to them by the dictionary administration.

5.8 Distributed Transaction Processing

This is a requirement for the workstation environment.

5.9 Hardware Independence

The rule talks in terms of a DBMS and this would not be applicable in the distributed development environment, it is the data dictionary / CASE input and output routines that need to comply. Here the work being done by ISO on Information Resource Dictionary Systems (IRDS) and the European Community work on Portable Common Tools Environment (PCTE) will be very applicable. There is however a need to ensure that the current conflicts between these standards are resolved.

5.10 Operating System Independence

The rule talks in terms of a DBMS and this would not be applicable in the distributed development environment, it is the data dictionary /CASE input and output routines that need to comply. Once again IRDS and PCTE will be important, but in addition the concept of Open Distributed Processing (ODP) may provide the answers.

5.11 Network Independence

This is a requirement for the distributed development environment.

5.12 DBMS Independence

The rule talks in terms of a DBMS and this would not be applicable in the distributed development environment, it is the data dictionary/ CASE input and output routines that need to comply. In the case of IRDS there is a services interface standard being proposed that would cover this area. It is at present a PASCAL binding.

6   CONCLUSIONS

Information Technology has been faced in the Eighties with the problem of not being able to deliver the applications that end users need. The software crisis is well known. Developments by the software vendors to tackle this problem have in the main been to aid the programmer and sometimes the designer. But it has been the analyst who has had little help and has in fact needed the most. Fourth-Generation Systems have provided a suitable solution for the design, coding and testing stages of the Systems Development Life-Cycle. This is particularly true when these pieces of software have been used in conjunction with prototyping techniques.

To produce good systems, IT needs to have them analysed and designed properly. Mainframe data dictionaries in the early 1980s were not found to be well suited to supporting the analyst. The analyst needs a tool that provides:

- graphics to cope with different methodology diagram techniques, such as entity relationship diagrams, data flow diagrams and functional decomposition charts;

- text manipulation, to allow the documentation of entities, attributes and processes.

Mainframe graphics has always been a problem in terms of performance. Therefore the birth of the corporate micro-computer was seen as providing the necessary environment for the tool to support the analyst. Thus, over the last few years, there have been a large number of products developed to exploit this environment and answer the problem of helping the analyst.

However, rather than solve the problems of IT completely, they have helped in certain parts, but at the same time created new ones. These problems include the following:

- Current PCs not being powerful enough;

- The need for a central dictionary;

- The booking in/out problem;

- Version control;

- The generation of code for foreign environments.

What is needed is a new generation of CASE tool! These new generations of CASE tools must be able to support the following concepts.

Firstly, as development is not a one person task, they must provide support for a distributed development environment. This can either be achieved by one vendor provide a tool set from PC through minis to mainframes, or by vendors collaborating. As a user I prefer the latter as it provides freedom of choice. However, to achieve this, there is a need for standardization not only for exporting and importing data definitions between dictionaries, but also for graphics and text. The needs of IT and the software vendors are crying out to be serviced by what appears to be ineffective standard bodies.

Secondly, the new generation of CASE tools must provide a means to support the whole of Systems Development Life Cycle (SDLC). At present, CASE tools provide support for the building of new applications. But it is common knowledge that approximately 70% of an IT department's time is spent on maintaining and enhancing existing applications. Our new generation toolset must include a Reverse Engineering Component to enable capture of existing systems into the methodology style of the CASE tool. The full support for the SDLC can be provided by one vendor, or a combination of tools from different vendors.

Thirdly, the new generation of CASE tools must allow the user to determine which code - be it COBOL or 4GL, which DBMS and for which machine. In addition I can see in the not too distant future the capability of simulating different operating environments on the development platform. The days of complete mainframe development are gone, and we shall see the use of PCs or Minis increase as the alternative development platforms.

Fourthly, I see the new generation of CASE tools exploiting rule-based technology. We already have Systematica's System Factory which allows the tailoring of the workbench to support the rules of any methodology. What is further needed is the concept of expert and naive use of the tool set. Naive users need to be given options as to what needs to be done, thus making them more productive. Expert users wish to be able to get right to the point they want to deal with. Computer Associate's IDEAL provides the sort of facilities I am talking about.

Fifthly, our new generation of CASE tools must support complete Version Management. The BSI IRDS panel have put forward a possible meta-model to provide the necessary support. I am not completely convinced that the model is what IT requires, and with a recent customer I have developed slight variations which we believe better serves the requirements of modern IT departments. Figure 11.11 shows the data model we have put forward.

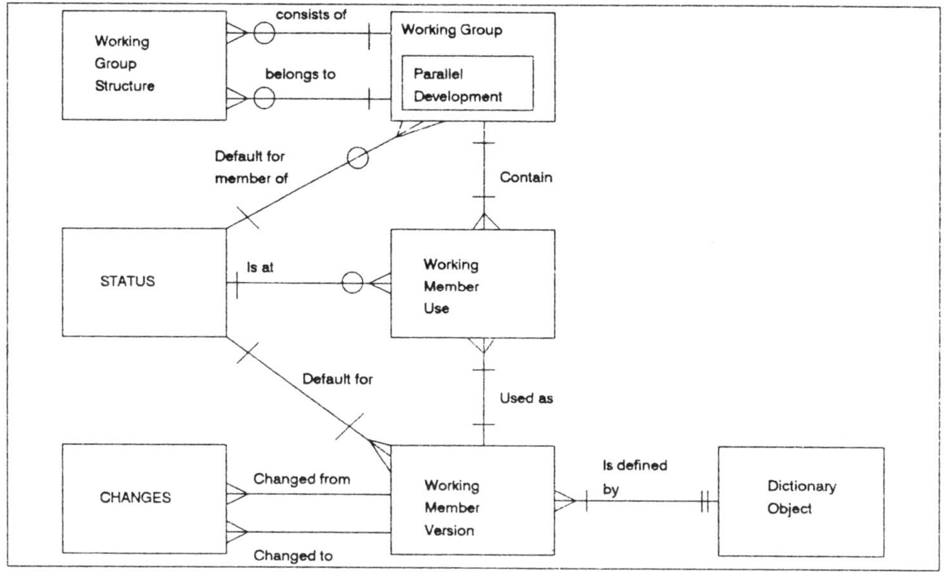

Figure 11.11 : Alternative meta model for version management.

Status is the object that allows the quality control states of the SDLC to be used to freeze or unfreeze definition. Changes in the object that allows only the differences between version to be recorded rather than complete copy of the Working Member Version.

Finally, the new generation of CASE tools must provide a complete and comprehensive solution to the booking in/booking out problem. Current tools provide some basic booking mechanisms. Examples are Excelerator and IEW. In my view, we need something much more sophisticated. If we use the example in Figure 11.6 to help illustrate what I see as the requirement. The first concept that is needed to be supported is that of custodianship of the meta-data. For many years, Data Management has talked about and tried to implement custodianship of the Data Resource amongst end-users. What we need is to apply this concept to IT. Let us say, that Designer C is the custodian of the Customer Database. If

Analyst A comes along and requests a copy of the database for update, the systems should log the booking out with or without a lock as is deemed appropriate. It should then automatically electronically mail the custodian, Designer C and Data Managment of the request. This will allow these individuals to contact Analyst A to find out what is happening. If Analyst B now comes along and requests the same version of the Customer Database, there should be 2 different actions. Either because the definition is locked, the access is refused and Analyst B is informed that Analyst A is in the process of doing an update, or the access is allowed but with the message that tells Analyst B about Analyst A. How much more user friendly this scenario is! And look at all the additional control that there is!

To conclude, current CASE tools offer IT the first automation of the analysis and design process of applications building. To increase IT's productivity for the Nineties, we need a new set of CASE tools which exploit knowledge-based technology. The human interface to the workstations will allow not only text and graphics but also voice. The challenge is there; we need to accept it!

REFERENCES

1   Trick or Treat?, Neil Holloway, ICP Business Review, Nov/Dec 1987.

2   Version Control with CASE in a Distributed Environment, David Gradwell, Notebook, Computing, 17th November 1988.

3   What is a Distributed Database System?, Chris Date, Relational Database'87, Codd and Date Limited, Dec 1987.

12

OOPS AND CASE TOOLS

Jon Lansdell
Bacchus and Smith Ltd

1   WHAT IS OBJECT ORIENTED PROGRAMMING ?

A definition of Object Oriented programming is :

> "programming by defining objects, their interrelationships and their behaviour".

Object Oriented Programming Systems (OOPs) are different in concept to conventional, or procedural languages, such as Pascal or C. OOPs consists of five main concepts: Objects, Methods, Classes, Message passing and Inheritance. The terminology used may vary between languages, that used in this paper will refer to the 'pure' OOPs environment of Smalltalk, but other languages, such as the object oriented extensions to Pascal or C will have different terms to describe the same idea. In a procedural language, there is a separation between procedures and the data which these procedures act on. In an OOPs language there is no distinction between an object and its data. An object may be looked upon as an extension to a simple record structure, containing not only fields but also the methods, the procedures which process it. An object's procedures are invoked by passing that object a message.

Classes are groups of objects of a particular type and all objects must be an instance of some class. Objects that are instances of a class , have the same structure, the same messages to respond to and the same methods available. In a drawing program, for example, all the rectangles would be grouped together in the class TRectangle, all the ovals in TOval and so on. Methods such as draw and writetodisk could be defined for each class, so that, for example, each time an object belonging to the class TOval needs to be redrawn, the particular piece of code which draws an oval is invoked. OOPs provides a programming structure which eliminates many of the IF/THEN and CASE structures which are found in many programs written in procedural languages and provides an ideal way of identifying commonality in systems.

In Smalltalk, when the classes are defined, the messages which can act on an object of this type are defined. These messages are linked to the methods which they invoke, for example when the message 'frame' is sent to an object of a particular class, it may call that objects 'drawoutline' method.

2   INHERITANCE

Probably the most important concept in Object Oriented Programming is that of inheritance. Objects are organised in a class hierarchy, with children inheriting methods and data structure from their parents. The classes on a lower level can access the data and methods of the higher level objects. To explain this concept, we can use the example of a drawing package, such as Macdraw on the Macintosh.

Designing a program of this sort using object oriented techniques, the designer could define a class TShape from which is the ancestor for all other classes. The TShape class would include rectangles, lines, circles, pictures and any other supported by the drawing package. Often its is the case that there is a lot of standard code used when drawing a shape of a particular type, writing that shape to disk, moving or resizing. A certain amount of this code is, however, specific to a particular shape. For example, when writing a the data for a circle to disk, the TShape class method can deal with writing the details of the structure such as the bounding box, as this will be used by all shapes. The TCircle method will need to override this method, inherit the code from the TShape class to write out the standard data and add some specific code to include information such as the radius.

3 THE ADVANTAGES OF OOPS

By using the techniques of inheritance and overriding, it is possible to make a large amount of code reusable, not just within the same application, but across a number of programs. It is possible to build up a library of methods which can be used in a number of different applications. Objects of one class can inherit code from a standard method before or after adding code specific to their own class, reducing the amount of code which needs to be written when a new class is added. OOPs applications thus become easier to maintain than ones written with conventional languages where similar code needs to be written as a special case for each new type of object added. OOPs techniques also make it easier to produce structured designs, because they force programs to be more modular in style and therefore make developers spend longer at the design stage of an application, resulting in a better product. The modularised nature of OOPs applications also makes them easier to debug, with most of the code relating to one object or process being located in the same place.

4 APPLICATIONS FOR OOPS

One of the uses of OOPs is in the area of simulations. Objects can be used to model real world entities and be designed to respond to messages passed to them. OOPs has been used successfully in applications such as financial modelling, modelling of social trends and more recently as a means of software testing. OOPs provides the most natural way of modelling the real world. Another OOPs application is that of real time systems, most of which are 'event driven', responding according to the messages sent to them. Machines like the Apple Macintosh are said to be 'event driven', responding to the user actions, whether it be moving the mouse, pressing a key or inserting a disk. This metaphor can be extended to support the modelling of complex real time systems.

OOPs is also used in graphics applications, particularly drawing packages, where there is a lot of commonality in functionality between different types of shapes, for example. Another common OOPs application is that of the user interface, the significance of which will be discussed later in this paper. OOPs can also be used for rapid prototyping of systems, being an ideal way to try out ideas on the interaction between modules in an application.

5   OOPS DEVELOPMENT ENVIRONMENTS

Simula is claimed to be the first object oriented language. Developed in Sweden and, as its name suggests, first used as a simulation language, it does contain a number of object oriented concepts but is not a pure OOPs language like Smalltalk. Smalltalk was developed at PARC and is not just a language but a complete environment and philosophy. Originally, because of its resource intensive nature, implementations of Smalltalk were restricted to mainframe and minicomputers, but recently a number of micro based versions of the environment have started to appear. Smalltalk is still not a language for developing stand alone applications, but it is an ideal prototyping environment.

The OOPs explosion has really been motivated by the hybrid languages, the object oriented extensions that are provided to languages such as Pascal and C. This allows developers to become familiar with using object oriented techniques and still use a familiar language. One of the most innovative of environments is MacApp. MacApp is Apple's library of routines written in Object Pascal to support most of the Macintosh user interface. MacApp provides a set of 'building blocks' from which developers can build applications, preventing them from reinventing the wheel and allowing them to concentrate on the detail of their own programs.

C++ is gaining in popularity and, because of the use of C as the language for portability across systems, is likely to be the standard for object oriented development in the future. There are also a number of other object oriented extensions available, including extensions to Lisp, Prolog and even Logo.

6   DISADVANTAGES AND MYTHS

As with any new method of programming, there are some disadvantages to using OOPs. The main disadvantage is that because OOPs is so different to conventional languages, there is a learning curve to be overcome, which can actually be greater if the programmer has years of experience with procedural languages. Some of this problem may be overcome by using a hybrid, an extension to a familiar language. Another disadvantage is that OOPs is not suited to all applications, particularly those of a smaller scale. Those new to this method of programming are advised not to try to write every application in an object oriented way, especially low level programs. With small applications there may be a code size overhead, but this of course gets less of a percentage of the total program as the application gets bigger.

There are some myths about OOPs which should be explained and dispelled. Developing using OOPs does not in itself produce larger programs, there may be a certain size overhead, especially when using libraries like MacApp. When the application gets more complex and the designer is able to use the concepts of inheritance and reusability, the OOPs application will probably be smaller than the one developed using a procedural language.

The other myths are that programs written using an OOPs are slower and more difficult to debug. There is a performance penalty for using techniques such as inheritance, but this balances with the better design that is achieved overall in an object oriented system. A badly designed program written using procedural languages is likely to be much slower. As for debugging, object oriented programs are often easier to debug and when an error occurs it usually only has to be corrected in one place.

7 OOPS AND THE DISTRIBUTED DEVELOPMENT ENVIRONMENT

There are certain specific problems involved in developing object oriented systems in a distributed environment. The first is the effective means of communication between members of the project team. The nature of object oriented design means that a change made by one team member will have an effect on the work of all the others. A CASE tool must support linking together the work of the team members and use the design methodology to determine the changes that will result from modifying the class hierarchy, for example.

The other problem with OOPs and the distributed environment is the integration between stages of a project. As will be discussed later in this paper, there needs to be an effective link between the deliverables of the analysis phases of a project and the processes that are involved in an object oriented design.

8 METHODOLOGIES FOR OBJECT ORIENTED DESIGN

In an object oriented design, as in most methodologies, the first stage is to specify the problem. The next stage is to define the user interface, which is especially important when modelling a system using a WIMP interface. Apart from identifying any usability problems at an early stage, doing the user interface design early makes it easy to identify objects such as menus, windows and palettes. The objects then need to be identified and these objects grouped into classes. The designer then builds a class hierarchy by identifying commonality and defining which classes should inherit the other's methods. The process of identifying commonality to deign reusable code can be termed 'incremental development' and will be performed a number of times until the most efficient design is reached. The object's interfaces to the outside world are then defined, which consists of the messages and methods. From this structured outline, all that needs to be done to implement the system is to write each method.

There are a number of formal methods for object oriented design, including : HOOD, GOOD, MOOD and OOSD. HOOD (Hierarchical Object Oriented Design) is perhaps the best known and is used in the design of systems using Ada, mapping directly onto Ada concepts. GOOD (General Object Oriented Development) is also oriented towards Ada, supporting the requirements and design phases of the development lifecycle. Data Flow diagrams are used for specifications and 'abstraction analysis' is used to transform the information in these diagrams into object diagrams for the design phase. MOOD (Multiple Object Oriented Design methodology) is another method under development. OOSD (Object Oriented Structured Design) is the design methodology developed at Interactive Development Environments and supported by their software through Pictures CASE tool. OOSD is not fixed to any particular language and can be used to support structured programs in conventional languages. It provides support for Inheritance, Classes and all other OOPs techniques and is intended to support libraries of objects to allow for code reusability.

9   USING OOPS TO BUILD BETTER CASE TOOLS

The techniques of OOPs can be used to build better CASE tools which can themselves model object oriented design. CASE tools generally support many diagram types and there is a commonality between the diagram functionality. OOPs can be used to provide efficient support for many diagram types allowing new types to be added without the addition of significant amount of code. OOPs also provides a structure for customisation, both by the user and by the programmer at a later date.

Data Modeller is an example of a CASE tool developed using object oriented techniques, written using Object Pascal and MacApp for the Apple Macintosh. The object oriented version supported five types of diagrams, with a large amount of common code and customisable symbols for each object. The object oriented version of Data Modeller provided three times the functionality of the original version written using conventional languages for almost the same code size.

Some object oriented environments, Hypercard and Allegro Common Lisp, for example, allow even greater user extensibility. Users can change the environment and the interface and do things that the designer never thought of. The CASE tools of the future must be designed for open architecture to allow users to customise notations, rules and interface.

10   OOPS, CASE AND USER INTERFACE

One of the many areas of computing that Smalltalk influenced was the user interface, lending many ideas to the WIMP (Windows, Icons, Mouse and Pull down menus) interface now found on many machines. In MacApp the Macintosh interface is modelled in the way that everything is an object. A window is an object that knows how to resize itself, to scroll it contents, a text area knows how to respond to mouse commands and keystrokes. Similar ideas are being used in other environments and the WIMP interface itself is spreading into several variants. The WIMP interface can be found under Microsoft Windows and Presentation Manager which offer a message passing architecture which is almost object oriented. X-Windows, News and the Next Workstation and many others now use the WIMP interface.

Another important concept that Smalltalk provided was the importance of the user. The single most important component of a computer system is the user. It is no use having a fully functional system which is impossible to use. There are many tools appearing which help developers with user interface design, some even generating code. For example, on the Macintosh, tools like Prototyper allow the creation of a prototype user interface which can be run in a shell. C or Pascal code can then be generated to implement the interface on the Macintosh. These type of graphical tools will replace code generators, lower CASE tools. Environments like NextStep on the Next workstation offer a graphical object oriented development environment.

If a CASE tool is to be used to build a system which will run under the WIMP environment, it must support user interface design and object oriented design. User interface design should be integrated into the rest of the project lifecycle and should be done as early as possible in the course of a project.

The standard WIMP interface provides benefits for both users and developers. Users can enjoy a consistent user interface across hardware platforms while for developers it opens up the possibility of using CASE tools for cross development. Using a CASE tool that supports user interface design can provide developers with portability and hardware independence and can be used to design for several different platforms at the same time.

11   ANALYSIS TO BUILD : THE GENERATION GAP

This paper has described the problem that exists in deriving an object oriented design from the deliverables at the analysis stage, translating the 'what' to 'how'. If CASE tools support object oriented design then the Entity Models and Functional Decompositions that were delivered at the analysis stage can be linked in a central dictionary with object diagrams drawn for the design. Diagrams can be checked for consistency ensuring that objects created are defined in some form in the Entity Model diagram, for example. Full CASE tool support for an integrated object oriented design method would make it easier to have a large team working on an object oriented project.

There is a caveat to this solution, however. Object oriented design methods are still in their infancy and while CASE tool support for them will be beneficial to developers it will not provide a complete solution. For example, none of the formal design methodologies consider the place of user interface design. If CASE tools are built to support object oriented design, as the more customisable ones can, then we will see better, more efficient systems built to specifications. The resulting systems will be easier to maintain and update. Integrated CASE tool support for User Interface design opens up even more possibilities and is vital for modelling systems with the WIMP interface.

12 CONCLUSION

We are heading towards an object oriented future. The challenge to the CASE vendors is to build better CASE tools to build better systems.

13
HOW CASE TECHNOLOGY
CAN PROVIDE
PORTABLE SOLUTIONS

Richard Barker
Vice President - CASE, Director Business Systems Division
Oracle Corporation (UK) Ltd

1 INTRODUCTION

Most companies of any scale now have a minimum of three or four different computer hardware suppliers. Even within a single vendor's offerings, the range of computers available varies from the not-so-lowly personal computer to the awesome parallel processors of today. Is it any wonder then that data processing departments across the world are demanding the capability to build their systems on one machine and yet be able to run them on any other they have available today - or in the future?

This chapter looks at the portable implementation technologies of today and then discusses how CASE technology can help to provide portable systems.

2 WHAT IS A PORTABLE SYSTEM?

In one sense it is the ability to physically carry an entire, useful personal system around, perhaps doing useful work within its own capability and possibly having the ability to network into other computer systems for more extensive processing. This is not the subject of this paper - but is worth a passing mention as it is now possible to have a 386-based lap top with virtually unlimited memory and a large hard disk to run say OS/2, Presentation Manager, a wordprocessor, CASE, the ORACLE Relational Database Management System and application software. The analyst and designer's dream of two or three years ago can now be fulfilled by such a portable workstation.

The sense in which the remainder of this paper is written is the sense in which the user or software engineer can write a program on one machine and run it **unchanged** on another. The ultimate in this is the ability of the program to relocate itself to an appropriate hardware platform, responding to the user as needed. This ultimate is exemplified by the ORACLE programming language PLSQL, which is not only portable code but can self-generate packets of code that can be transmitted across a heterogeneous network to run elsewhere - an essential concept for a truly distributed database.

The industry, however, recognizes that 'C' is the most portable opportunity open to most software engineers of today. When combined with portable fourth-generation tools and SQL from ORACLE, available on over one hundred hardware environments, software engineers can now write very portable software.

These mechanisms are no panacea. The 'C' language is very rich, and extreme care has to be taken to use constructs that work in all environments. The SQL database access language may be found from many vendors, but few offer the compatibility required for this strategic task.

The diagram below (Figure 13.1) illustrates a typical distributed and portable solution being built today.

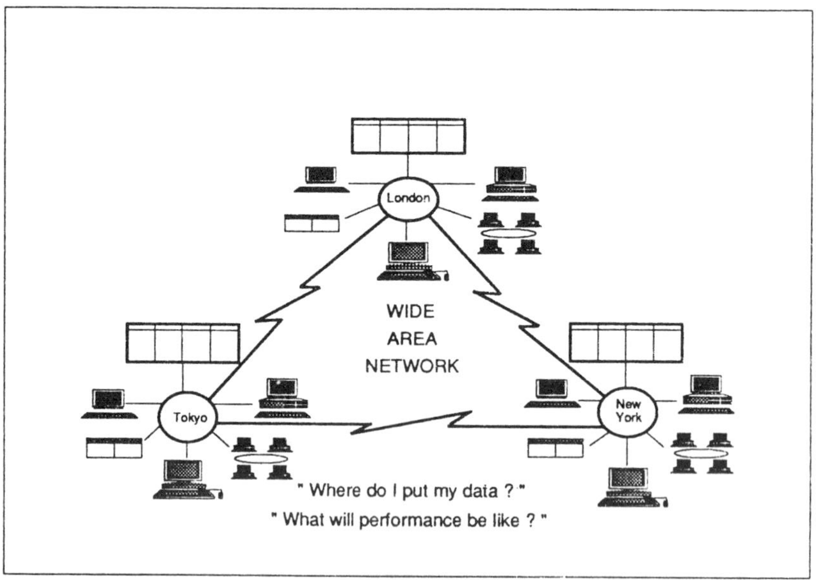

Figure 13.1 : Distributed databases and processing networks.

162

Here we have a heterogeneous wide area network of computers, each of which may be supporting a local area network. Personal computers, workstations, mini and mainframe computers are coexisting such that each supplies the particular functionality, performance and usability required. Locally, specific machines may be offering facilities such as word processing, whereas all users of the network have access to a common set of applications - within some form of security and access control umbrella.

The concept of portability in this case includes the ability to interconnect machines transparently for electronic mail, distributed processing and distributed database. Portable, high-usability applications may be run on some chosen machine, for example, a PC, and yet access data anywhere on the network. Other high-performance, transaction processing applications may be run from any form of terminal or workstation to run against some powerful mainframe. New hardware, from a wide variety of alternative vendors, can be added at any time to meet new demands.

So far we have only discussed the implementation vehicle. How do we know what we should be building for our end users and how it will perform?

The answer is embodied within the framework of Computer-Aided System Engineering and its associated methodologies.

CASE consists of several components, each of which supports some form of life-cycle method for developing a system, and project management and control to optimise the use of the resources deployed. The software components of CASE then comprise an integrated software tool set as follows:

- distributed multi-user dictionary or repository

- analyst/designer workbench

- database and application generators

- 4GL and decision-support software

- project control and management capability

Let us briefly have a look at the main components of CASE and how each can contribute towards providing portable solutions.

3   A LIFE-CYCLE METHOD

CASE tools are designed to support some form of structured method which guides the developers through the stages of building a system. A typical life-cycle is illustrated below(Figure 13.2), with each stage having clearly-defined tasks which must be carried out and deliverables necessary for subsequent stages.

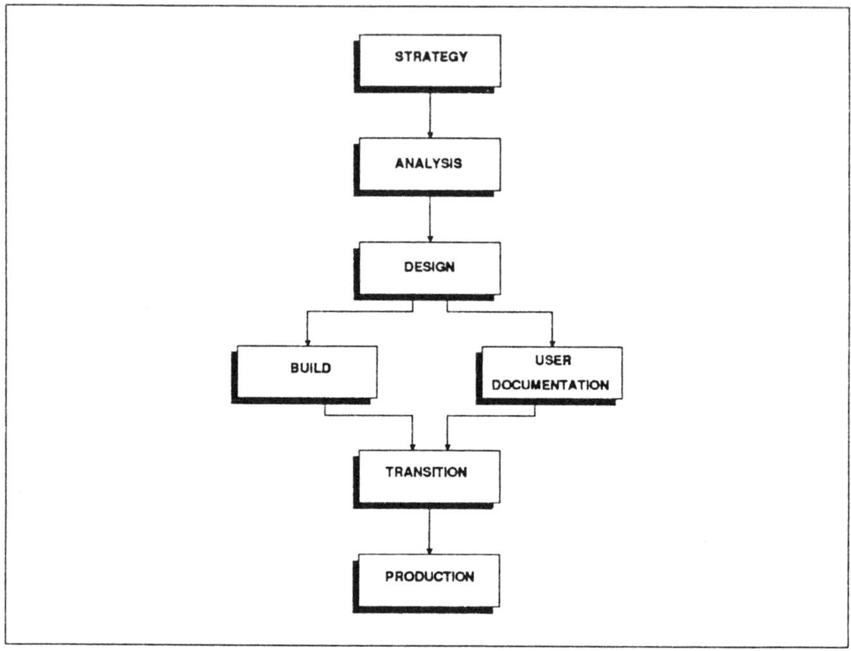

Figure 13.2 : An example of a typical life-cycle.

The need for portable solutions will tend to evolve during the strategy stage. Interviews conducted with key executives across a geographically-dispersed organisation may unearth a distributed pattern of working - possibly across several countries with different language, legislative and cultural requirements.

Feasibility during this stage will address currently available technology and potentially available hardware, software and networking capabilities. Some technology strategy may already be in place, perhaps including a multiple vendor policy.

164

These business requirements and technology opportunities are brought together within a new strategic plan, encompassing a possible systems architecture, development approach and detailed, phased, costed development plan. These plans **must** be within the context of a clear understanding of the business direction, stated in terms such as objectives, aims, critical success factors and priorities. With one company, for example, they were moving from a centralised organisation towards a de-centralised customer orientation, which was reflected in a technology solution that started on a mainframe and then evolved to a fully-distributed interactive network in several countries. A clear case for highly-portable solutions in all senses.

During analysis, the detailed functional and information requirement must be defined. Distributed requirements must be categorised by geographic location and operating business unit to answer questions such as, *"What functions are carried out where, and how often?"* and *"What information is held where and how much?"*

During design, detailed feasibility of alternative solutions is considered, resulting in the design of the database (possibly distributed), application processing (again possibly distributed), network architecture, security and access control, and interfaces to existing systems both computerised and manual.

During the build stage the entire system is put together and tested, hopefully using some of the portable tools available. ORACLE Corporation, for example, provides a portable database environment, fourth-generation languages for forms, queries, reports, menus and even a fully-portable electronic mail capability with programmatic interface.

Transition is when this possibly complex solution is pulled together, tested as a whole and conversion made from existing systems. And finally the production stage is where the real benefit of the portable solution can be made available to the end user.

Let us now look at the CASE software that assists this process and some of the specific tools that can help.

4 DICTIONARY OR REPOSITORY

A prerequisite for any CASE software is a multi-user, preferably distributed database in which to hold the requirement definition, design and ultimate system. In the so-called **Upper CASE** area the interlinked concepts of functions, dataflow, datastore, entities, attributes, relationships, domains and events are maintained. For these distributed requirements it is also important to record the details of the geographically-dispersed business units and their need for information and functionality.

At the end of analysis, completeness and consistency reports should be available, which in this situation should include the perspective from each business unit.

Utilities come into play to bridge the gap to the **Lower CASE** area, with its files, tables, columns, programs, and processing nodes. Database design utilities should be followed by optimisation facilities and sizing predictions. It is at this stage that the concept of a logical schema with possibly many physical implementation schemas becomes important, where each target implementation may be separately tuned for different requirements. And even there, things change and version control becomes an essential feature.

5 ANALYST/DESIGNER WORKBENCH

The systems engineer, whether an analyst, designer, data administrator, programmer, and so on, ideally should be accessing the data held in the repository via some form of multi-user, multi-tasking, multi-windowed workstation, which integrates the use of all his CASE and other software tools. The use of rigorous diagrammatic techniques, which interactively update this shared data, is now the accepted standard. In addition to the expected dataflow, function hierarchy, entity relationship and other diagrams, the workbench should include sophisticated matrix diagramming capability by which means one can record, check and finalise the usage of:

- data by functions

- data to file or table

- function to program

- file/table by program

and for distributed requirements

- data at location

- functions carried out by business unit, leading to

- programs at processing unit.

The diagram below(Figure 13.3) illustrates the use of a matrix diagrammer to define the initial mapping between business functions and distributed business units. Subsequently, details would be added for frequency of use and possibly the change in usage pattern over time.

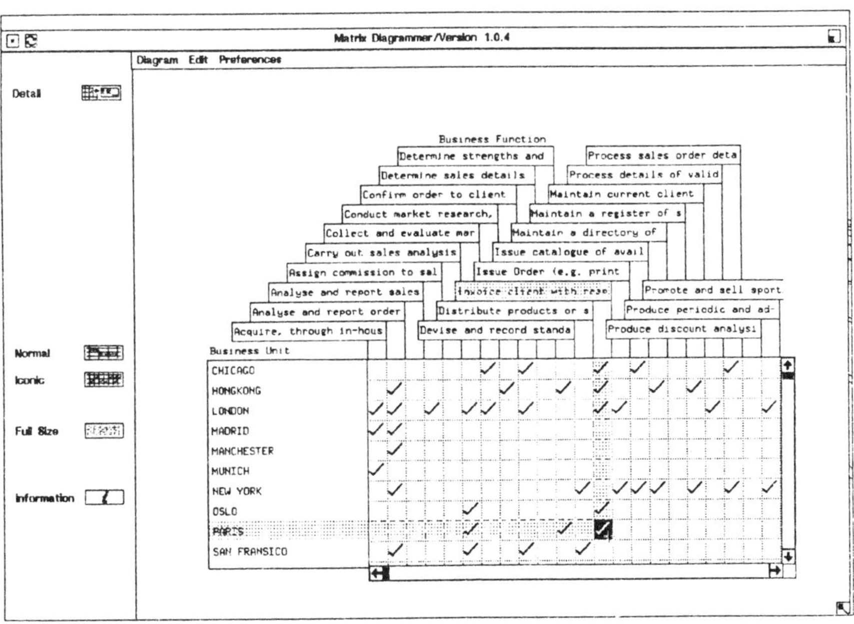

Figure 13.3 : An illustration of the initial mapping between business functions and distributed business units.

Few CASE tools have evolved to diagrammatically represent the target distributed database/processing heterogeneous network.

6   DATABASE AND APPLICATION GENERATION

Having stored the logical and physical database design within a development machine environment it is not a large step to generate the Data Definition Language (DDL) for the target machine, for say an ORACLE, DB/2 or other database management system. Control must, of course, extend to subsequent changes of requirement.

But the real application portability comes from taking the dictionary definition of **what** a business function must do, the characteristics of the target machine environment and the features of the chosen implementation language and then being able to press the button to generate the application. Two forms of application might resuly. The first is a program that can be run **without** change on many compatible machine environments; for example, with the ORACLE SQL* Forms system on say UNIX, VMS or PC. In other cases, the target environment may make it necessary to change the **way** in which the generated program works - for example, if the target environment utilised a block mode as opposed to a character mode terminal.

Portable programs, as generated by the above mechanism, still require further work, as there is no way any automated tool can tailor the look and feel to the precise needs of an individual or the way a particular group of people may need to work. The benefit of generating fourth-generation language programs is that user customisation can typically be achieved very quickly.

168

7 SO WHAT HAVE WE FOUND?

CASE can help identify distributed requirements and gives us a complete picture of the functional and information needs of different business units in the organisation.

CASE can help take one logical database design and produce multiple physical designs for different target machines.

CASE generators can take one functional definition and produce either portable code or code tailored for the specific operational conditions.

8 PORTABILITY FOR CASE ITSELF!

Similar requirements are to be found in the development area where the database this time is a CASE Dictionary/Repository and the portable code this time consists of the diagrammers and utilities that comprise the CASE applications. ORACLE has also built a portable CASE development environment where the dictionary may reside on the machine of your choice and the workbench on the workstation of your choice (e.g. SUN, HP, VAX station, OS/2 and PM, ...) Further, where the CASE application is via a textual interface, the terminal may be block mode, character mode or bit mapped, as required. Needless to say such a CASE tool is built using itself.

9 WHAT DOES THE FUTURE HOLD IN STORE?

Work is going on in many areas

At the user interface, emerging technology is already allowing you to write the code for a logical device, and the interface layer automatically adjusts for Presentation Manager, DECWindows, OpenLook, and so on.

At the database layer, 'gateways' and 'connect' interfaces will enable you to write to industry-standard SQL, whilst the software provides a gateway to the target DBMS.

At the generator level, the use of style templates and user-defined preferences will gradually remove the need to tailor the generated programs. And when the target language is replaced, simply re-generate your portable code to the new one.

Exciting times are ahead for the advocates of portable code.

14
THE ROLE OF CASE
IN IT COMPETITIVE STRATEGIES

Robert Magee
Independant Consultant

It's taken over a quarter of a century for us to apply our own computer technology to the design and development of Information Systems - an eventuality that many of us consider long overdue.

Coincidental to the emergence of CASE technology, the business world has realized the value and potential of "Competitive Strategies" in dealing with rapidly changing market forces. The secret to success for a handful of companies and individuals has now become a *de facto* standard for the increasing majority of commercial, or commercialy orientated organizations.

In today's highly competitive business world the ability to be first on the market, or at least very close behind the leaders, is a key factor in virtually all commercial successes. In turn, this need for prompt and effective responses to competitive threats and opportunities has placed increased pressure on the IT function. Without CASE it is difficult to see how the IT Manager could maintain a sustained response to these new and more urgent demands for systems and information.

Whether CASE was simply a very good idea somewhat late in its arrival, or a product born out of necessity, maybe a moot point - but what is true is that systems have historically taken too long and cost too much to develop. If we can achieve all of the benefits from CASE that we should, then there will be many more application systems that are delivered on time and within budget.

This in itself will be a major contributor to the overall competitive position of the company.

Over and above the ability to provide a rapid, cost effective response to demands for new systems and services, many IT managers see the need for a broader and more direct involvement with the company's Competitive Strategies.

At a minimum he/she will gain advance notice of impending changes that will impact the IT function.

Not surprisingly therefore, the "IT Strategy" of the past, which was for the most part a series of policy and operating statements, has given way to a new phenomenum, the "IT Competitive Strategy".

Recognizing that CASE is a systems engineering facility and that it is the availability of information and application systems that will have the most direct impact on the businessman's ability to compete effectively, our focus should in the first case be towards those needs rather than towards hardware and software architectures or IT organizational and service strategies.

Before getting carried away with the impression that in using CASE in a competitive context we are using completely new tools to address a new concept, we should remind ourselves that the methods and techniques embodied within CASE technology have been used with much success for many years - both in systems planning and development contexts.

Competitive strategies have existed since the very beginnings of trade and commerce and the competitive instinct has its roots in the earliest contests for food and territory. However, with the possible exception of strategies in the military context, it is only recently that we have given the subject such detailed, formal attention and publicity. Given that before long just about everyone will have a competitive strategy, those with the greatest committment and implementation skills will undoubtedly be the real winners.

In order to broaden our understanding and to establish a context for IT's involvement in the company's competitive strategies, it is well worth taking the time to revisit those key issues and concepts that are applicable to any planning venture. In so doing we should remind ourselves that, although an unplanned and unstructured environment may provide many moments of intense personal satisfaction when our energies, skills and talents are successfully deployed under extremely adverse conitions, there is an underlying feeling that one of those heroic dashes through the minefield may prove fatal.

There may be less individualism and fewer medals in a well planned compaign, but, as an organized and unified force we can achieve far more than our heroic counterparts. In the process we will also show a far more efficient, effective and profitable deployment of available resources.

A plan defines the method by which specified goals and objectives may be attained, more typically, a plan defines the changes to be made to an existing method in order to accommodate new or modified goals and objectives.

It is also generally recognized that goals and objectives are predominantly modifications of those set for prior plans. The nature and extent of the modifications being determined from the degree of success or failure experienced in preceding periods of operation and knowledge of the methods employed in those same periods.

Details of existing methods and procedures must be provided as input to the planning process in order that the changes necessitated by new/modified goals and objectives can be identified and described.

The ability to combine experience with a knowledge of existing methods is the most important feature of any planning process. The setting of goals and/or development of plans without this ability must be regarded as a speculative and experimental enterprise.

In contrast to this, there is far less risk and uncertainty involved in a planning process that relies exclusively on historical performance data and detailed knowledge of current systems and procedures.

In the same context, the quality, accuracy and completeness of both historical performance data and of existing processes and procedures will have a direct impact on the quality, accuracy and completeness of plans made using that information.

In the business environment, corporate goals and objectives will determine the overall Functional and Administrative structure of the company (Organization) and its principal Processes and Procedures (Systems).

Where the practice is continued through to the design of individual organization units and individual systems it is a relatively simple task to synchronize those developments thereby maintaining high levels of consistency and objectivity.

Without this discipline there is a strong tendency for individual elements within the total organizational structure and systems environment to evolve at different rates and under different conditions.

As with any evolutionary process there are as many different end results as there are influences on the process itself. In the business environment the overall impacts are reduced effectiveness, efficency and consequently reduced profits.

The benefits of planning are only felt when the efforts defined by that process are implemented, and when the results of efforts under a particular plan (or group of plans) are carefully measured and recorded for use in future planning exercises.

In conclusion it can be seen that planning is a structured, hierarchical process that is largely dependant upon the quality and availability of information about the subject organization, its functions, structure, systems, procedures and capabilities.

Putting it simply; a strategy must have realistic goals and objectives. Implementation of a strategy will in all probability have far reaching effects on the organization and its systems and, most importantly, what you did yesterday is the best starting point for future endeavours.

In terms of the use of CASE in support of competitive strategies, the most important contribution the IT junction can make is to provide a comprehensive and complete picture of the company, its business and information systems and its information/data resources. The IT function with its objectivity, analysis skills, ability to think logically in abstract or conceptual terms and its involvement in projects throughout the organization, is uniquely qualified to undertake this task. CASE with its charting, cross-referencing and repository features etc, seems to be the ideal tool to deal with large volumes of information and complex relationships.

Building a model of the company, its functions, process and information will however be a severe test of IT's level of understanding of the organization as a working organism. It will also test the understanding that different line managers have of each others operations and issues.

174

In developing such a model, bear in mind that the businessman's horizons do not stop at the office door or factory gates - neither should your picture of the company's operating environment. External relationships, communications and information are arguably much more important than internal diagnostics. Consider for a moment the Marketing/Sales functions - they should be at least equally concerned with issues such as; consumer disposable income, socio-economic trends, market geo-demography and competitors product and pricing strategies. In most companies there is precious little of this type of information but plenty of historical data to tell us what have been the results of market changes.

Similarly, at the opposite end of the supply chain, we have traditionally focused on the book-keeping aspects of purchasing and materials management. Very few companies have invested equivalent amounts in formal systems to measure and analyse, for example, supplier delivery performance, material quality failures and availability of free stocks or spare capacity at supplier locations - All of these things have a direct relationship with our ability to deliver our own product on time and within quality/price parameters acceptable to our customers.

In other words, your CASE model must not only be complete in terms of the company's internal position, but it should also reflect the broader business environment. By definition it should therefore include; interfaces to external entities forming part of your supply and distribution chains, customers and markets, and your competitors. In addition, there are other classes of external relationship, which, although not obviously of direct competitve value, are nevertheless often very important. Sources of financial and human resources, legislative of govermental bodies and affiliated companies within a group are typical examples of these secondary external relationships.

Obviously a model of your company and its business environment is likely to be fairly large and complex. You will therefore need to work at high levels of summarization using conceptual/logical definitions and descriptions rather than detailed specifics. Particulary at the highest levels of your model you are likely to find that processes/functions and information look very much alike i.e. the boxes on your charts labelled "Marketing", "Distribution", "Purchasing", etc could equally well refer to those subjects as functions or databases.

Given that your company is organized on a functional basis and that management recognizes activities better than logical data groups - the basis of the model should be functional and the primary communications between IT and the user communities should be via process flow diagrams and functional hierarchy charts. Once common ground has been established there is nothing wrong with using data flow diagrams, however information analysis, subject databases and the like will probably be regarded at best as "interesting" and quite clever".

Whilst on the subject of IT/user communications and before looking further at the CASE model and its potential uses, we should take a few moments to consider two major issues that are likely to impact your ability to work effectively with senior management.

Firstly, many companies are now implementing a number of competitve and management concepts including; Value Chain Analysis, Critical Success Factors, Total Quality Management, Effectiveness Areas and Corporate Missions/Objectives. As IT practitioners with aspirations of becoming more intimately involved with competitive strategies we would be well advesed to gain at least a basic understanding of these subjects.

In terms of their impacts upon the company generally and IT in particular, you can expect to see requests for systems and information that cut across established functional and organisational boundaries. These requests will, in all probability be less well defined then their predecessors. This is due in part to the fact that they relate more to a concept or philosophy than to physical events, and also to the fact that many managers from a variety of disciplines will all be trying to get to grips with new ideas that require them to work as a coherent management team.

The champion of such enterprises is likely to be the chief executive or a senior board member. As is traditional, he/she is not usually available for detailed discussions and is equally unlikely to be the Project Manager/Co-ordinator - (Perhaps the IT manager might like to volunteer his analysis and project management expertise).

176

On a cautionary note, if your company is not undertaking one of the above or something like it, are you sure that you (IT) can convince them that they should be or that you really should have an "IT Competitive Strategy"?

This leads us to consider a second issue, and that is the credibility of the IT function as a partner in, or contributor to, the company's competitive strategy.

One of the most common complaints amongst IT managers concerns their ability to convince management that they can do much more than deliver computer systems. In other installatons, IT has elected to develop its expertise in the technology rather than the business it supports, leaving management to identify their specific needs. Where these, or similar circumstances exist you would be well advised to take back seat, or, if you have the courage of your convictions, to mount an IT Marketing / PR campaign to establish your credentials and your desire to participate more fully in the management of the business.

In the latter situation, CASE might prove to be a sufficiently novel concept that it has a lot of value as a marketing tool. There is nothing quite like a well orchestrated demonstration of computer wizardry (with all the bells and whistles playing) when it comes to getting management's attention. Bearing in mind also that you get a lot of attention when you deliver mediocre systems late and over budget!. Even when your best efforts have overcome horrendous technical design and development problems, including the lack of user involvement at critical stages, it is still the users perception of your overall performance that counts. In many ways IT has its own "Price Value Perception" problems to deal with in the same way as Marketing /Sales people do in dealing with your Company's customers. No matter how good you think the product is - you still have to deal with your customers perceptions of what it should be. Once again CASE might prove very useful if you can demonstrate (or create the impression) that you are now able to deliver a quality product faster and cheaper.

Having dwelt a little on these somewhat sobering issues its appropiate now to rekindle our enthusiasm for CASE in a competitive context by examining some of the principal uses of a model of the company and its environment.

Starting close to home you should have little difficulty in identifying and recoding all existing application systems and their attendant data mangement systems. Having done this you will be in a position to examine your systems and information portfolios with the objective of determining your proximity to (or distance from) a competitive systems environment. In basic terms this is achieved by classifying the contents of the portfolios according to the degree to which they support your customers and supplier, front-line functions, support activities and accounting/administrative functions.

By expanding your model to include all of the company's main functions, processes and data flows you will be able to repeat the portfolio analysis treating manual systems and documents in the same manner.

In both of the above exercises the value of your findings will be greatly enhanced by the inclusion of quantative measures (or realistic estimates) of the manpower, operating costs etc. Without this added dimension a function box with one or two associated staff looks the same as an activity requiring two hundred!.

It is also very enlightening when you overlay your current IT coverage onto the total company model: gaps in support to specific functions or along particular processing chains become very apparent. You should not be too discouraged when you find that there is little or no support for the customer or your Marketing/Sales functions and that over 70% of your systems are directly attributable to accounting or the accounting aspects of line functions.

At this point in your analysis of your competitive posture you will not only have a good insight into the evolutionary processes that formed your current environment but you should also have created a partially prioritized list of IT systems development opportunities.

In those situations where the company has established its goals and supporting strategies, you should be in a position to evaluate the extent to which existing systems will support management plans and to identify those areas which will require further development.

Where the IT function has traditionally been closely involved with business operations and management you may be able to adopt a more proactive posture and use the CASE model and your analyses to point out deficencies and opportunities - highlighting their relevance to the business and quantifying their impacts. Bearing in mind earlier comments regarding the extension of the CASE model to include external relationships information etc., this would be a good opportunity to combine technical knowledge and expertise with competitive ambitions in the creation of IT scenarios that embrace your customers' and/or suppliers' needs.

Assuming that something positive happens as a result of your company's competitive strategies, the CASE model becomes an invaluable IT planning tool. It should be reasonably easy to assess the impacts of new systems and information requirements and to identify existing data and functionality that might be further exploited.

In concluding this review of the "Role of CASE in IT Competitive Strategies" there are a number of issues worthy of re-iteration. Firstly, without a sound corporate Competitive Strategy you are unlikely to get very far with your IT Competitive Strategy.

Secondly, a good understanding (and demonstration) of your existing company and IT positions is essential to line and IT management in the development of meaningful strategic plans.

Thirdly, CASE, at a minimum will help IT deliver better systems more quickly and economically. Optimally CASE can be a valuable tool in the development of functional, systems and information models of both current and future environments.

Finally, in terms of support to the development of competitive strategies, CASE is only a tool. Without the right attitudes, culture and analysis skills it has no place or purpose. Your biggest problem will be in creating the environment and circumstances in which its powerful features and capabilities can be effectively deployed.

15

DATA DICTIONARIES IN A MIXED ENVIRONMENT

Richard Francis Williams, PhD
Independent Consultant

1 INTRODUCTION

1.1 The business need for sharing data in tourism in Western Europe

Many organisations are involved in tourist activities in varying contexts. These centre on the needs of travellers to be aware of facilities that are available in places that they wish to visit. All tourist travel is based on the availability of accurate information being provided on all relevant aspects of the places of interest. This includes the various options of travel type, accommodation and facility availability, and the required prices and times associated with them.

The information that is collected is done so by various parties. These are generally undertaken by organisations advertising locations to their best advantage. This is particularly true of national and regional tourist boards and tour operators, whose primary purpose is to attract visitors in large numbers to specific places.

However, in Western Europe there are a number of other information gatherers. They are both independent of the needs of national and regional economies, are not attempting to sell a definable product, and place the interests of the tourist at the top of their priority list. These information gatherers include touring clubs, who collect information to support the needs of their members. The members tend to be independent tourists wishing to be flexible in terms of the places that they visit and stay at on any particular vacation. To support such requirements the clubs have collected information on all aspects of potential interest to the independent tourist. These vary from accommodation details and features to visit, to the legal and environmental details of the places to which the tourists tend to go. Information on the quality of many of these items, (notably accommodation types), is included, so that the members can have a degree of confidence on the facilities referenced.

Since many clubs in different Western European countries were undertaking similar activities for their respective members, senior touring managers felt that a degree of unification and standardisation in these matters would benefit all concerned. The member would have access to more detailed and wide ranging information over a geographically larger area, and the clubs could rationalise the costs of data collection and maintenance, if it was undertaken in a concerted and centralised manner.

Three clubs became involved in such a unified initiative, (from The Netherlands, The Federal Republic Of Germany and The United Kingdom). Others were contacted to discuss their interest in the idea, and a number of positive responses to this approach were received. This extended the potential for co-ordinated touring information collection and provision in the future. The European Commission in Brussels also signalled its interest in the project, as one of its objectives is geared to attracting northern European capital, into southern European economies. Tourism is one such area which is of primary benefit to southern European countries in terms of their overall economy.

Positive responses to the initiative were also received from North American and Australasian clubs and organisations, and a prototype and the project were instigated by the three initial clubs, examining information on France. Most independent tourists that travel between northern and southern Europe pass through France. As France has no club of a similar level to the three project sponsors it was regarded as a logical starting point for the activity in business terms.

1.2 The strategic business requirements of the major partners in the project

In strategic terms, the business requirements of the project were relatively easy to determine. This is because they had to reflect the expanding needs of the tourist industry and allow the concept of The Single European Market in 1992 to be reflected in the project. They can be classified as follows:

- That the results from the project provide a standard of agreement on international definitions for data of interest to tourists. This must include hotels, camp sites, national regulations, restaurants and travelling conditions within its scope.

- That both dynamic and static data must be catered for within the project. Static data is unlikely to require amendment more than twice per year, but the dynamic data, on items such as road information, is subject to change on a quarter hourly basis in some cases.

- That the standards of inspection of places and features must be uniform, allowing data quality to be guaranteed.

- That whilst the project would initially involve only three partners, it must have the flexibility and capacity to expand to include any number of further partners in the future, without significant technical difficulties.

1.3 The development context of the project : technical environments

Whilst the strategic business requirements of the project were easy to determine, the development itself had to reference a number of other problems. These can best be described by examining the technical environments of the primary participants. Whilst all three clubs were significant mainframe computer users, the actual architecture of each was strikingly different;

- The German partner was a large IBM mainframe user, employing Adabas as its database management system, and Data Manager as its data dictionary.

- The Dutch partner, whilst also being primarily an IBM mainframe user employed Datacomm as its database management system, and the ADR dictionary product Datadictionary to support it.

- The United Kingdom partner compounded these differences by being an ICL mainframe user, with IDMS-X as their database management system, and the ICL data dictionary DDS.

Hence, in machine hardware and software terms the clubs exhibited almost as much difference, as they did similarity in political and business will. The mixture of the three types of newer, (post hierarchic), database management systems were exhibited, (inverted list, (partly) relational and network), all running different dictionary environments.

Thus, there were a number of likely problems in terms of the recording and control of the information that was produced.

2 THE STRATEGY OF ANALYSIS AND DOCUMENTATION OF THE PROJECT

2.1 Analytical and documentary requirements and problems

It was a fundamental requirement for the successful development of the project that all work undertaken on business data definition be done so in business terms, and be business, rather than data processing led. The reasoning behind this approach is standard in all systems developments. It assures that the project sponsors can retain the logical control of the developments direction. In this case these needs were even more clearly necessary:

- Because of the potential risks of misinterpretation or understanding in respect to the different natural languages of the participants in the project.

- Because the final solution, and its implementation is required to be ported to other, different machine environments, and natural languages outside the three types exhibited by the initial participants.

These two primary requirements were hampered in technical terms by the lack of existing standards relating to the definitions of data dictionaries, into which the information was to be stored, and from which they were to be transferred to other such facilities. There currently exists no recognised international standards for data dictionary content and connections. Although recommendations for standardising dictionary content and meaning are currently being worked upon, even these "standards" are subject to division. Work on the development of a set of Information Resource Dictionary Standards (IRDS), is being undertaken in Europe and Australasia, whilst in North America ANSI are undertaking separate work in the same field, which may not be directly compatible with the IRDS work in its outcome. Coupled with the fact that it may take well into the 1990's to produce such a set of standards that suit the requirements of many users, dictionary standardisation is a major technical restriction to such developments.

2.2 A documentary strategy proposal to support the project needs at the present time

It would be more effective in technical terms to wait for the production of a set of recommendations for dictionary standardisation in respect of at least one of the bodies currently working in the area. This is not possible given the fact that the business requirement for the system is current, and not a number of years away. It is also important to appreciate the very nature and environment of the project in terms of its geography, and its consequent political profile. To produce an achievable recommendation in this context was also a necessary requirement. In an attempt to categorise the likely problems associated with data distribution the documentation of the analysis of the project was decided to be used as a prototype of the projects implementation, given the existing problems in this area.

The strategy that was produced to support this concept reflected both the political and physical aspects of the project, as well as its technical and logical needs. The outcome was as follows:

- The central physical location of the project was determined to be in West Germany, and consequently it was recognised that distributed working must be possible in the other two countries.

- That as a result of this decision on location, the central repository for the documentation produced was to be Data Manager, which was the local, West German, dictionary. In this respect the other two dictionaries became its "slaves" for the duration of the analysis.

- That interfaces between the recognised "master" dictionary and its "slaves" needed to be produced internally within the project to allow distributed work on the business data definitions to be undertaken. As IRDS interface recommendations in this field do not yet exist, the resulting software developed to support the activity had to be produced and maintained by project personnel rather than the dictionary vendors.

- That only one natural language was to be used for the project, and that all work was to be undertaken in that language, which was determined to be English.

- That the analytical approach adopted was entity modelling and its associated activities.

- That communication between the dictionaries was to be via a unified network of PC interfaces, rather than by directly linking the dictionaries together in a truly distributed manner. This was because of the problems of the lack of vendor support and lack of standards in interface definition terms in this area.

These aspects of the strategy could be said to be sub-optimal in a number of ways in respect to a truly greenfield distributed development. This is accepted by both the business users and the technicians involved in the project, but it was felt to be the most simplistic strategy that could be developed which had the most effective chance of success. Its adoption would also enable a view on the implementation of the working system to be obtained. Consequently the distribution of dictionary data in this manner could be used as a true "prototype" to identify any physical or logical difficulties, discrepancies or omissions in the strategy before it was placed before business users in a production context.

2.3 The implementation of the strategy : data definition development in a distributed environment

The manner in which the process of international data definition development is being undertaken in this project in a distributed environment is quite representative of the problems currently exhibited by many such activities. Its very nature is truly open system in every sense, and as little or no vendor support exists for the activities, the most simplistic implementation of the strategy must be adopted. In this case the following activities occur:

- Copies of the Data Manager definitions are distributed over the PC network for parallel working on them to take place.

- All amendments are subject to date and time stamping to ensure the continuity of definitions.

- The actual definitions to be worked upon at the distributed sites are booked in and booked out manually by the three personnel responsible for data administration at the distributed sites.

- All amendments are returned to West Germany for inclusion in the central documentation on a weekly basis and uploaded back into the main dictionary.

- All distributed data transfer and communication is undertaken by the network, including data administration in terms of the authority for individual definitions to be worked upon at any of the relevant sites.

The administration of the distributed data definition development is undertaken in the most objective and controlled manner possible, given the lack of software support to actually achieve it automatically. In physical terms the PC interface ensures a degree of communication and access control to the data definitions. The relevant internal formatting and reformatting activities to load and unload the definitions into and out of the distributed dictionaries follow simplistic rules in terms of the times of the week at which they are allowed to happen.

2.4 Data distribution limitations on the project.

As can be seen from the strategy and its implementation, the distribution of data across the three sites is somewhat labour intensive and slow. Many significant limitations on the level of distributed activity that can occur currently exist, and these can be summarised as follows:

- The whole process is batch in its implementation, no real time data definition work sharing is possible.

- The interfaces between the dictionaries and the PC network are internally produced, and non-supported by the respective dictionary vendors.

- Consequently the interfaces are passive in terms of their relationship with the dictionaries. Any changes to the interfaces require changing manually, as does the production of the code to achieve them.

- Translation into Dutch and German is not catered for by the strategy or its implementation at all.

- The problems of administering the data definitions will be compounded by the addition of new partners into the project.

- The lack of standards direction, and consequently software vendor support for such data distribution activities means the whole process is in its infancy, and will remain there until such time than international agreements upon standardisation can be achieved.

3 DATA DISTRIBUTION AND THE FUTURE

3.1 Specific future distribution support requirements for the project

Given the fact that no likelihood of international standards recommendations for an IRDS are likely to be forthcoming for a number, (if not many), years, it is important at the level of the project, to identify what extra support requirements could be satisfied from one source or another in the interim. In response to this realistic view of the distributed environment in international contexts a set of specific requirements for the support of the actual distributed data instances and their definitions must be proposed that takes account of this situation. Martin [1], recommends that if the technology cost permits, it is best to store the data where they are to be used. In this case the project would require multiple copies of the data to be kept at the respective sites of primary use. It is envisaged that all three primary partners in the project will have numerous requests for data access, and so it is essential that access is as easy to achieve as possible. Many reasons for the implementation of copies of the data exist in terms of the project. They can be best summarised as follows:

- It is likely to become an expensive activity transmitting many responses to requests for data over the network, especially since the network is not owned by the clubs involved in the project.

- The response time for data access will be reduced if the data is stored at each of the primary sites.

- The data is more readily available, and is less likely to be at risk from destruction if more than one copy exists.

- The data will be able to be organised to suit the local requirements of the primary partners data processing environments, and given the fact that each of these is significantly different from each other at the moment, this is a major benefit.

All of these points are important business reasons for producing multiple copies of the data of interest to the business as a whole. It is the current opinion of the technicians on the project that such a situation will unquestionably occur, especially when one includes the significant extra point of the actual financial importance of the data to the business. By accepting this set of circumstances as being both likely, and financially desirable for the future benefit of the business, a set of data distribution rules and controls for the successful implementation of the requirements must be developed. Consequently, mechanisms must be introduced to the environment to ensure that they are achieved, even if they are not the most dynamic methods of their implementation that could be conceived. As has been seen by the example of the physical constraints and limitations placed upon the distribution of work on the development of the data definitions within the project, the necessary controls may be rather simplistic and arbitrary:

- That data creation and update authority for certain data types be constrained to specific applications/locations.

This would ensure that data integrity is maintained. It is a current view of the development personnel that the best implementation of this aspect of the actual production strategy will be achieved by different primary project members maintaining the instances of values for different data types (entities). It may translate into the situation where the Dutch would maintain information on features such as museums, while the Germans maintained camp site data and the British maintained data on hotels, for example:

- The relevant data of interest to the different partners would therefore be able to be transmitted across the network in a controlled manner.

This would ensure that inconsistency and protocol overheads were minimised. The approach would also assist in recovery, as valid points within the databases could easily be returned to after any significant database failure:

- This situation would reduce storage overheads as well as increase the likelihood of accuracy and audit control over the data being achieved.

- In essence the database would become partitioned, and for most users, would be a simplistic replicated database, due to the fact that most of the data held is relatively static, (unlikely to change more than once per year).

In these cases any third party request for data could be easily met from any one of the the primary sites "copy" of the database. The aspects to which any individual party is responsible for, in terms of maintenance could be accurate across all of the distributed sites on the same time scale that is currently true of the distributed data definitions, (ie once per week). Third party queries would only be allowed to reference the static copies of any data of interest to them, ensuring the integrity of the reports produced. In the case of the proposed example, while the UK partner was responsible for hotel data maintenance, any query relating to hotel information would be satisfied by one of the other two partners, in terms of an external or third party enquirer.

The only problem with this simplistic approach to data distribution in the specific case of the project relates to truly real time, or dynamically changing data. In this business situation such dynamic data relates to actual road traffic information and hotel room bookings. In this, and other such real time situations various pragmatic choices for the projects implementation are currently possible to envisage:

- Accept that the data in this context is likely to inaccurate, or only able to reference long term information, (such as major road-works, and their likely, or historical impacts on traffic at certain times of the day, week, month or year);

- Accept a much higher cost in providing information on these matters in a less structured manner (ie by telex);

- Accept that true synchronisation of real time data will be subject to a margin of error, (of at least an hour or more).

For most users, inaccuracies of an hour or two are not crucial. If one is stuck in a traffic jam however, then this can be argued as not to be the case. Currently, no other realistic alternative in this context is available. This is because the technology necessary to support such a requirement for greater accuracy is not yet commercially available. In this respect one must look into the more distant future to support the true requirements of any commercial real time distributed environment.

3.2 General future distributed data support requirements

To properly support any real time distributed data environment, it is essential that a set of fundamental user requirements are met. These can be said to focus upon the following:

- For Open System Interconnection (OSI) capabilities to be widely implemented. This would allow easier communications between machines and software of different types to occur, regardless of the implemented data processing architectures that are existing within organisations.

- That IRDS standards, (or ANSI equivalents), linked into an OSI environment would enable any interested user to share the common data definitions that have been produced within a business area or project.

- That the Portable Common Tools environment, (PCTE) will be in existence to enable any interested organisation to have the capability to maintain, alter or extend any existing data definitions of interest to them.

- That true distributed processing can be undertaken, following the rules and guidelines of objective data distribution, as stated by Date [2]. This will allow real time distributed activities to occur and obey all of the integrity and consistency rules applicable within centralised database environments at the current time.

It is a widely held view that this final point will only be effectively achieved with the introduction of distributed relational processing capabilities. In such an environment the problems of deadly embraces within distributed databases, and processing will be avoided. In the context of the project referenced within this paper, the only current way to implement the concept of two phase commit is by intervention by the respective data administrators across the distributed sites agreeing who has authority to undertake any individual alteration to a data definition of a particular point in time. In a production situation such a level of manual control would be unacceptable to all parties, and thus must be automated.

It is the stated aim of software vendors to achieve the level of distributed processing described in this section as necessary to achieve a real time environment of relevance to commercial organisations. From the point of view of the project referenced in this paper in such contexts, it is hoped that it will not take as long to achieve as is being estimated for the agreement of standards to support the concept of an IRDS. If it does, then business opportunities will be suboptimised, and some may never be developed at all.

4 REFERENCES

1. MARTIN, J. (1986) : Data-Planning Methodologies, Prentice Hall, New Jersey

2. DATE, C.J. (1987) : What is A Distributed Database System? Parts 1 and 2, The Relational Journal

16

AN ENVIRONMENT TO SUPPORT DISTRIBUTED DEVELOPMENT

Sami Zahran,
Senior Management Consultant, Digital Equipment Company Ltd

1 JUSTIFICATION FOR DISTRIBUTED IT INFRASTRUCTURE

Most large international business organisations are geographically distributed. This is due to a variety of reasons, for example, the spread of resources for manufacturing, distribution outlets, human resources availability, business mergers, diversity of business activities, ... etc.

The progress of Information Technology took a strong direction to support such physical distribution. This is evident in the convergence of the computing and telecommunications technologies, for example. Nowadays organisations can easily design and adopt a distributed IT infrastructure to reflect and support their distributed business topography.

A similar pattern is emerging in the area of applications development. The technology is actually here today to support a distributed development environment. In this paper we will discuss:

- Motivations behind distributed development.

- Topography types of development environments.

- CASE tools that support distributed development environment. This is supported by examples of how this is currently adopted by Digital Equipment Corporation.

2 MOTIVATIONS BEHIND DISTRIBUTED DEVELOPMENT

2.1 Geographic dispersion of development resources

It is natural nowadays to see a large system being developed in more than one country. For example, the specifications could be done at a corporate level in the USA, while the systems design could be performed in the UK, and the actual program development could be done in the Far East. The justifications behind these could be economic or relevant to human resources.

2.2 Dispersion of users supplying requirements

Large international organisations are normally spread geographically across several sites if not several countries. In many instances we will find the manufacturing function in one country while the assembly and distribution functions are in another, and the marketing as a local function in several countries. In order to develop corporate systems to serve such an organisation, the users who would define the systems, requirements will be spread all over the place.

2.3 Critical mass factor

This again could be one of motivation behind distribution. In some locations, there may not be enough critical mass to justify software development at this specific location. In such cases distributed development may be the only way to bring critical mass to a project.

2.4 Availability of technical resources

This relates to the first point, where a specific type of technical skill may exist at a specific location. This could motivate the distribution of specific development activities to be allocated where the best technical resources exist.

3 TOPOGRAPHY TYPES OF DEVELOPMENT ENVIRONMENTS

In order to design an architecture for CASE environment, we should study the topography of the development environment, then design a CASE environment to map or reflect such topography.

Generally there are three types of development environments:

3.1 The single developer environment

This environment refers usually to the development of embedded systems or small engineering and technical applications. A typical examples is an R&D environment where individual researchers each develop their own experiments.

Figure 16.1 illustrates a development environment that could serve a single developer. Usually this will comprise a PC or Workstation with all the appropriate CASE tools available to the developer. The Developer will have his own private CASE repository or encyclopaedia, where he stores all the development information. Such a CASE environment is sometimes referred to as a single-tier environment.

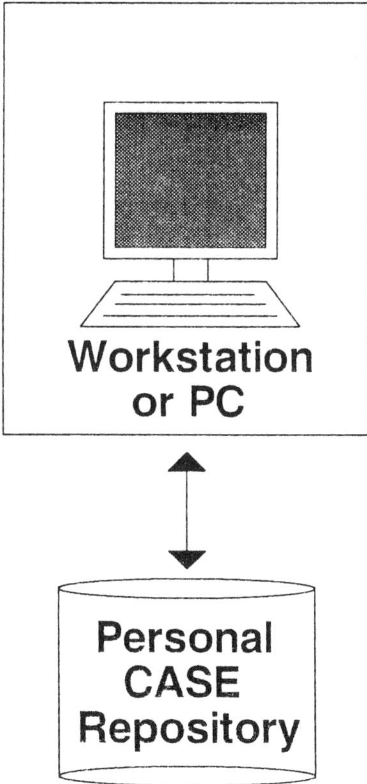

Figure 16.1 : CASE: The single developer environment.

3.2 Workgroup of project-team environment

This environment refers to the development of software packages or self-contained application system where the development will be undertaken by a team of developers usually located near each other. A typical example is package development environment in small software houses, where a team of developers will be dedicated to developing a specific software package.

Figure 16.2 illustrates a development environment that could serve a workgroup environment. Usually this will comprise a terminal device (e.g. a PC or Workstation) for each developer, all linked together via a local area network (LAN). There will be two distinct types of CASE repositories, one for the private repositories for each developer, while the other is the project repository for the whole project. This is sometimes referred to as a two-tier environment. Some of the issues to be addressed in this environment relate to what is called the booking-in/booking-out procedures necessary to ensure the consistency and integrity of the common repository.

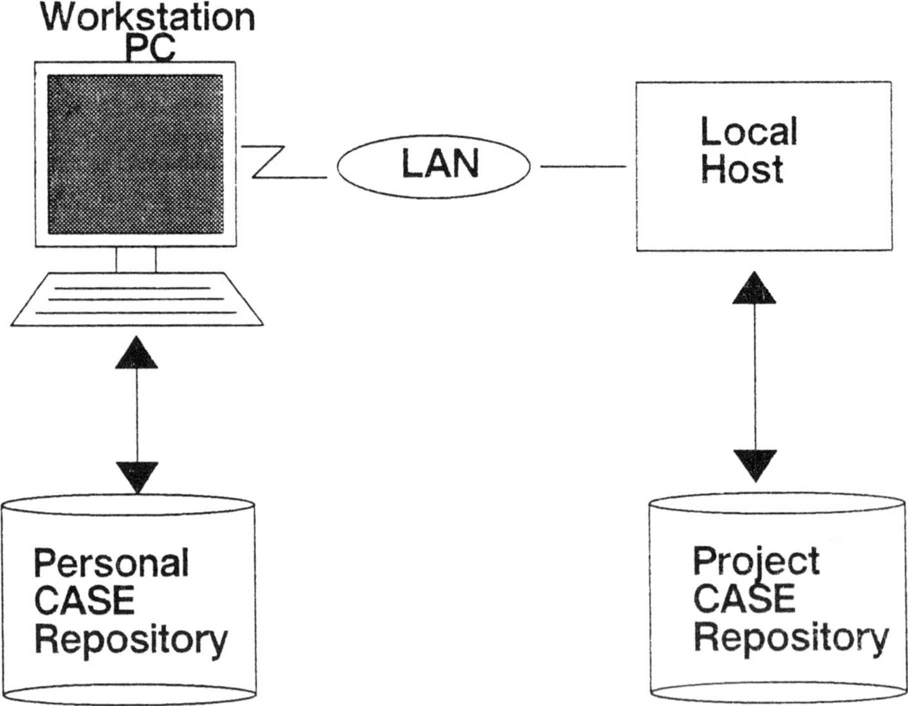

Figure 16.2 : CASE: The workgroup environment (two-tier architechure).

3.3 Hybrid or distributed development environment

This environment refers to the development environment that may exist in large, multi-function, geographically-dispersed organisations. In such environments there could be several teams in several locations, each developing one application system, and a central corporate function which coordinates the development and develop common systems that cut across several application areas. This environment is usually a mixture of the other two environments linked together via a local area network and a wide area network (WAN) to faciliate the communications among the different locations.

Figure 16.3 illustrates the development environment that could support this type of development environment. There are three levels of CASE repositories in such an environment, a single developer repository, a project team repository, and a corporate repository. Some of the main issues to be addressed in such environment are the procedures to ensure the consistency and integrity of the corporate repository and the project-team repositories.

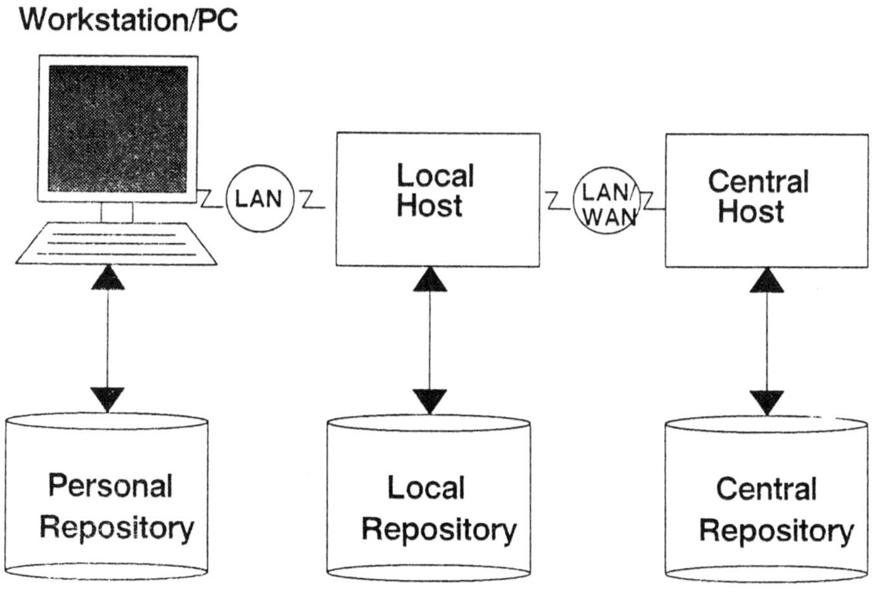

Figure 16.3 : CASE: The distributed environment (three-tier architecture).

The main networking technologies required to support such an environment would be LAN (e.g. Ethernet) and WAN technologies, as illustrated in Figure 16.4.

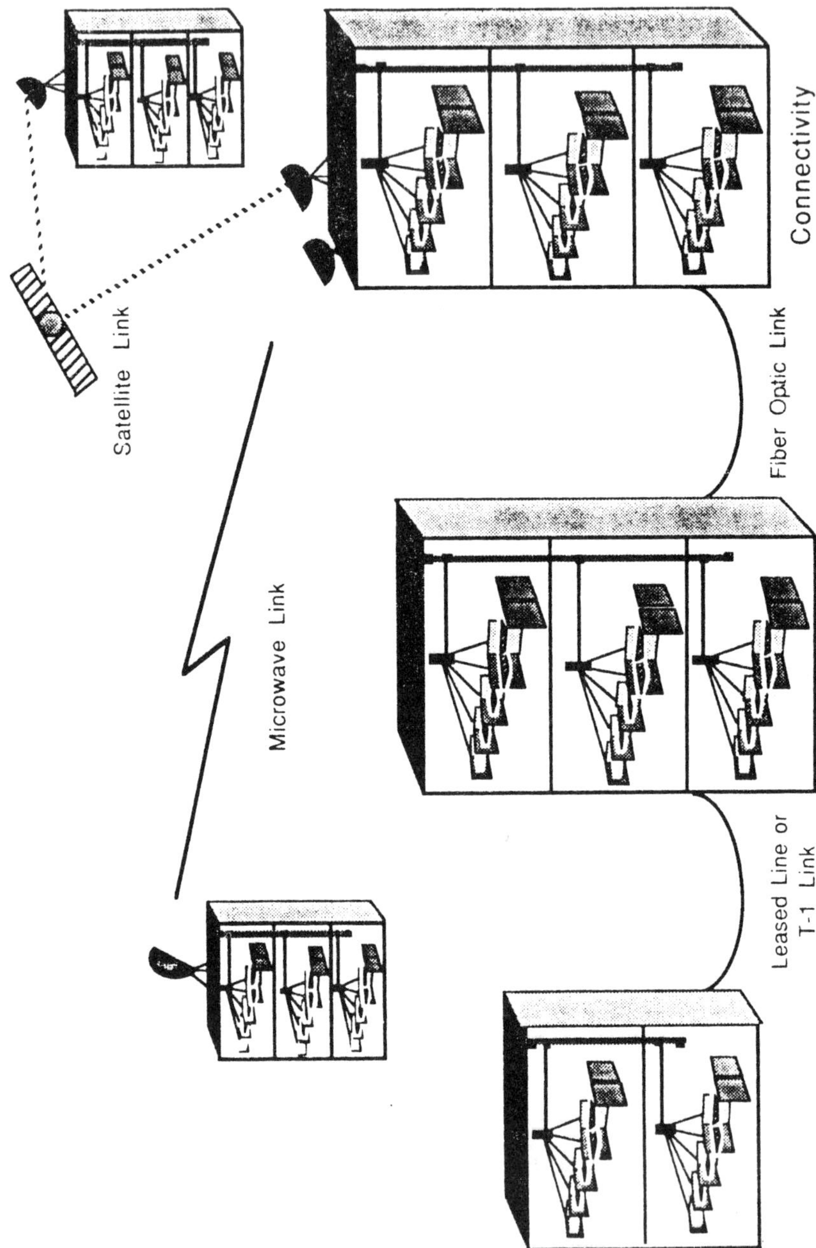

Figure 16.4 : Enterprisewide LAN: utilizing high performance bridges.

The main components of the infrastructure required to support these development environment are:

- Hardware Platforms, which may comprise desktop devices, local and central processing devices.

- Communications Platforms, which may comprise local area networks and wide area networks.

- Basic Software Platforms, which include operating systems, systems software, database management systems, TP monitors ...etc.

- Development CASE tools, which include CASE tools that support the different development activities for that type of environment.

- Support CASE tools, which include CASE tools that support relevant activities e.g. communications, documentation, project management, ...etc.

4 CASE TOOLS THAT SUPPORT DISTRIBUTED DEVELOPMENT ENVIRONMENT

4.1 Distributed CASE repository

An essential element for CASE environment to support distributed development is the CASE repository which can support the distribution. Digital Equipment offers its VAX common Data Dictionary/Plus (CDD/Plus) as a distributed, active, open architecture dictionary in order to satisfy the requirements of a distributed development environment.

VAX CDD/Plus can function as a distributed dictionary, uniting geographically separate organisational units (or develoment teams) by providing one logical dictionary system that is physically dispersed. A distinct advantage of VAX CDD/Plus is this feature whereby you may have many physical dictionaries, but a single logical dictionary across a cluster, a local area or wide area network.

Figure 16.5 illustrates different physical dictionaries in a VAXcluster.

Different physical dictionaries in a VAXcluster

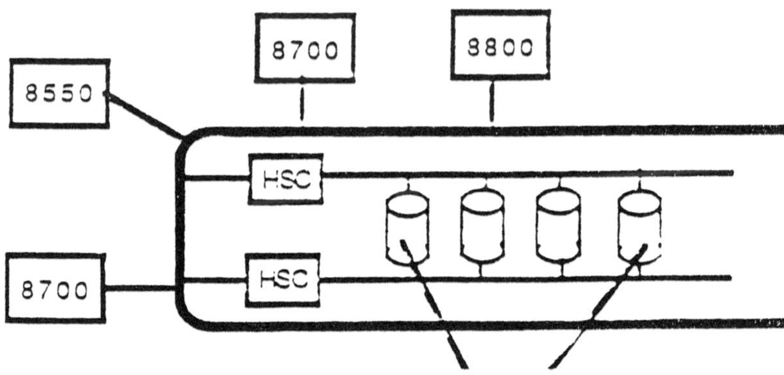

Figure 16.5 : Distributed VAX CDD/Plus.

To ensure the consistency and integrity of the meta-data, VAX CDD/Plus equips the data adminstrator with the tools to grant or deny specific access rights to dictionary definitions. Also to ensure the completeness, accuracy, and consistency, CDD/Plus provides journalling capabilities to automatically protect dictionary sessions from system failures.

4.2 Communications tools

The methodologies of modular, top-down application design is an aid to distributed development, because it makes it possible to assign responsibilities for particular components to particular development sites. However, communication and exchange of information between the different sites is still required.

The types of communications that may exist in a distributed development environment could be one-to-one, one-to-many, or many-to-many. Digital Equipment Co. offers a range of communications support tools that covers all these types as follows:

- Digital's networked VAX MAIL system supports one-to-one and one-to-many communications. This can enable communication between evelopers on geographically separate systems.

- Digital's VAX NOTES covers many-to-many communications through conferencing. NOTes conferences are a particularly effective way to collect user requirements and to faciliate communications among a group. Technical questions need be answered only once and user input can be directed to specific issues.

- Digital's VAX CDD/Plus enables sharing definitions across the network. It is ideal for maintaining data administration standards across the project. A data adminstrator can be given responsibility for data definitions, and other data adminstrators across the network can reference these elements within specific database or file definitions.

- Digital's VAX CMS enables networked access to code libraries. Being able to share code across the distributed development team is a tremendous aid to productivity. Through the use of Distributed File Services, VAX CMS (Code Management System) can provide remote access to code libraries.

5 SUMMARY AND CONCLUSIONS

Distributed development is now a reality. More and more business organisations will find themselves distributing their development process for one reason or another. Digital Equipment Corporation is already distributing the development of its software systems, and has a comprehensive set of CASE tools to assist and support this environment. These tools and products are available to Digital's customers to support their distributed development environment.